LIGHTROOM CLASSIC 2025 MASTERY

Pro Techniques in Lightroom Classic for Flawless Photo Finishing

SLOANE DELANEY

TABLE OF CONTENTS

INTRODUCTION

What is Lightroom Classic?

Lightroom Classic is a software created by Adobe, mainly for photographers who want to manage and edit their photos with a lot of control and detail. Lightroom Classic offers superior features to simple photo apps, allowing you to fine-tune your photographs without affecting the source files.

Among its primary functions is the easing of picture organization. Lightroom allows you to effortlessly organize and discover thousands of images by importing them, creating folders for them, and applying filters like ratings and tags. Large picture collections are now much easier to manage. To avoid reorganizing your photo library by removing related images from their original folders, you may alternatively create collections to store them in.

Beyond organizing, Lightroom Classic is known for its editing tools. Adjusting sharpness, contrast, color tones, and brightness are just a few of the many things you can accomplish. For more detailed adjustments, such as adjusting curves, applying effects, or dealing with selected regions of the image, there are even finer options available. The original picture will remain undamaged regardless of the number of alterations you apply since these changes are **non-destructive**. If you decide you want to try another style or change your mind, you can simply return to the original, unaltered form.

Lightroom Classic, in a nutshell, is an all-in-one solution for photographers seeking robust organizational features and extensive editing capabilities.

Overview of Adobe Photoshop Lightroom Classic 2025

Several significant enhancements to the photo editing experience are brought about by Lightroom Classic 2025. The new **Generative Remove** feature uses AI to quickly and efficiently eliminate undesired objects from photographs. Another notable addition is the enhanced **HDR support**, which allows for more streamlined processes for producing and exporting HDR images. Digital signatures on exported JPEGs are now possible with the inclusion of **Content Credentials**, and **Denoise** now supports more raw file types, including linear DNGs. Quicker camera identification is a result of improved **Nikon tethering**, and workflows are made easier with better library management.

New Features

1. **Generative Remove**

    The **Generative Remove** tool, which uses artificial intelligence to make object removal in photographs easier, is one of the outstanding features of Lightroom Classic 2025. Thanks to improved object recognition, this function makes it easier for users to spot and remove undesired things. Even with complicated or intricate backgrounds, the AI can detect the item with a simple brush, allowing for quicker picture editing without the need for precise human adjustments.

In the **Develop** module, select **Remove** ✏ > **Detect objects**.

1. Roughly brush over the object you want to remove. To get a more detailed selection, you can adjust the brush size.

    Note:

    To select the whole object, roughly brush around it.

2. The refine controls allow you to make the following selections once you've chosen an object:

    o   **Add** - Add areas to the selection.

    o   **Subtract** - Subtract areas from the selection.

    Inside the chosen panel, you'll find adjustments for the brush **size** and **overlay** color.

3. In the chosen panel, select the **Remove** button.

4. **Generative AI** powered by Adobe Firefly can be combined with **Detect objects** to analyze and automatically select the object and remove it for optimal results.

5. To cancel the modifications, choose **Reset**.

2. **Content Credentials**

With the new **Content Credentials** security feature in Lightroom Classic 2025, you can now attach digital signatures and metadata to your exported or shared pictures, ensuring that they are valid. By including crucial details like ownership and modification history, this upgrade protects your digital assets, making it easier to track and identify your photographs online.

3. **Denoise for Linear Raw DNGs**

The enhanced **Denoise** feature now works with linear raw DNG files, making it simpler to get clean, clear photos. Canon, Nikon, and Sony high-resolution raw files, as well as Apple ProRAW, HDR, and panoramic DNGs, may have their noise levels reduced with this feature. Even in dim light, photographers may now get sharper shots.

Open Lightroom Classic: Open Lightroom Classic and import your raw DNG files.

Go to the Develop Module: Navigate to the Develop module after selecting the picture you want to edit.

Select Denoise: Locate the Denoise section in the Detail panel of the Develop module.

Apply Denoise: After you click the Denoise button, Lightroom will begin processing the image. This will reduce noise while preserving details.

Fine-Tune Settings: If necessary, adjust the noise reduction settings to get the desired outcome.

4. **Optimized Tethering Support for Nikon**

   Lightroom Classic 2025 has **improved tethering support**, which is great for Nikon customers since it speeds up and simplifies the procedure, particularly with Zfc, Z9, and Z6 III models. Streamlined workflows and more efficient live shootings are the result of improved tethering architecture, which guarantees faster camera identification and import times.

5. **Expanded Camera and Lens Profiles**

   By continuously adding support for new cameras and lenses, Lightroom Classic ensures that it remains current with photography gear. Photographers can now use their newest gear with ease thanks to the addition of profiles for recently introduced cameras and lenses.

6. **Smart Albums for Better Photo Management**

   The new **Smart Albums** feature also helps photographers save time by automatically creating albums according to user-specified search parameters. By simplifying their picture management processes, users may save time with this tool's improved photo organization and search capabilities.

   Create a Smart Album: First, make a smart album by right-clicking the Collections panel in the Library module. Hit the **Create Smart Collection** button.

   Set Criteria: You may provide your Smart Album's parameters in the resulting dialogue box. Options include date, keywords, star rating, flags, and more.

   Name Your Album: Give your Smart Album a name that describes what it is and why you made it.

   Save and Use: To store your Smart Album, click **Create**. Then, you may use it later. If you specify criteria, Lightroom will automatically fill it with photographs that fit those requirements.

Smart Albums automatically arrange your collection without requiring any user intervention by updating themselves whenever you add or edit photographs that meet the specified criteria.

7. **Enhanced Develop Module**

   Better responsiveness and smoother navigation are two changes brought to the Develop module in Lightroom Classic 2025. This improvement makes it easier for photographers to apply modifications and transitions between photographs, which boosts productivity overall and is particularly useful during long editing sessions.

Additional Feature Enhancements and Improvements

- **Automatic Catalog Backup After Upgrade**: After upgrading to a new version of Lightroom Classic, the program will automatically generate a backup of your existing library. If you ever need to go back to an older version of the catalog, you can be certain that it is safely saved thanks to this function.

- **Simplified Catalog Renaming**: With this update, renaming a catalog is a breeze. By going to **File > Rename Catalog**, you can now rename your catalog without leaving the software, saving you time and effort. Managing enormous picture collections becomes much easier with this simplified procedure. It saves time and avoids mistakes.

- **Preview Cache Management**: You can now restrict the amount of your preview cache, which makes managing disk space more efficient. Users can choose the amount of storage space reserved for previews, which helps them avoid wasting space when dealing with huge picture collections.

- **Improved Performance in the Develop Module**: Lightroom Classic has made the **Develop module** more responsive, allowing for quicker and smoother picture edits. Users are now able to more easily navigate between photographs and make modifications, which greatly enhances their editing efficiency.

- **Expanded HDR Export Options**: The latest update introduces additional file formats with **HDR export support for ISO gain maps**. This ensures that the quality of exported high dynamic range photographs remains constant across platforms, giving photographers greater freedom in their work.

- **New Adaptive Presets**: Improve your productivity with the addition of many new adaptable presets. **Adaptive Sky, Adaptive Portrait**, and **Adaptive Subject** changes have their own set of presets that photographers may use to quickly and accurately apply creative effects.

- **HDR Support for Secondary Displays**: Lightroom now allows users to enjoy HDR material from several perspectives concurrently by supporting **HDR on secondary screens**. This is great news for those who work with many monitors. For photographers, the ability to see high dynamic range photographs on many displays allows for more precise editing.

CHAPTER 1

GETTING STARTED WITH LIGHTROOM CLASSIC 2025

System Requirements for Running Lightroom Classic 2025

Windows:

- **Operating System**: Windows 10 (64-bit) version 21H2 or later, or Windows 11.
- **Processor**: Intel or AMD with 64-bit support, 4-core or higher, with SSE4.2 or later.
- **RAM**: 8 GB minimum (16 GB or more recommended for high-resolution editing or large images).
- **Graphics Card**: DirectX 12 compatible GPU with at least 2 GB of video RAM (VRAM) is required; 4 GB VRAM or more is recommended for higher-performance tasks like using the Denoise feature.
- **Display**: 1024 x 768 display (1920 x 1080 or higher recommended).
- **Hard Drive Space**: 10 GB available space (SSD recommended for better performance).
- **Internet**: An internet connection is required for software activation, updates, and some features.

macOS:

- **Operating System**: macOS 12.0 (Monterey) or later.
- **Processor**: Intel or Apple Silicon processor (M1/M2 chips).
- **RAM**: 8 GB minimum (16 GB recommended for optimal performance).
- **Graphics Card**: GPU with Metal support and 2 GB of VRAM (4 GB or more recommended).
- **Display**: 1024 x 768 (1920 x 1080 or higher recommended).

- **Hard Drive Space**: 10 GB available space (SSD recommended).
- **Internet**: Required for activation, updates, and certain features.

These requirements are designed to handle common photo editing jobs. Working with high dynamic range (HDR), 4K video, or massive panoramas requires a more robust machine with more memory (RAM), a faster solid-state drive (SSD), and a graphics processing unit (GPU) with more memory (VRAM).

Downloading and Installing Lightroom Classic 2025

1. **Visit Adobe's Website:** Go to Adobe's Lightroom Classic page.
2. **Sign In or Create an Adobe ID:** To access Adobe products, either log in with your existing Adobe ID or establish a new one. Please log in if you have an account.
3. **Download Lightroom Classic:** Select **Download** to begin downloading Lightroom Classic. Additionally, the Creative Cloud desktop program will be installed on your computer if it isn't already there.
4. **Install the Application:** To install Lightroom Classic, open the file you downloaded and follow the on-screen instructions.
5. **Launch Lightroom Classic:** Lightroom Classic can be launched from either the Creative Cloud app or your desktop after it has been set up.

Why Use Lightroom Classic?

There are several important reasons why photographers and editors use Adobe Lightroom Classic which are:

1. **Non-Destructive Editing**

   You can modify your images in Lightroom Classic without worrying about losing any of the original files. With this non-destructive editing feature, you can safely experiment with various adjustments without losing any of your raw data because you can always return to the original image.

2. **Advanced Photo Management**

    With its powerful organizing and categorizing features, users can effortlessly handle thousands of photographs. Images can be easily sorted and retrieved based on specified criteria thanks to the ability to tag, rate, keyword, and create collections.

3. **Comprehensive Editing Tools**

    Lightroom Classic's extensive set of tools is guaranteed to please photographers at all skill levels, from those just starting to those with years of experience. Among these tools are advanced capabilities such as Generative Remove, HDR merging, and AI-powered Denoise.

    Local adjustment brushes, gradient filters, and advanced color correction are all part of the Develop module's toolbox for making precise modifications.

4. **Integration with Adobe Ecosystem**

    Thanks to Lightroom Classic's tight integration with Adobe Photoshop and Camera Raw, you can save time and effort by completing more involved modifications in Photoshop while keeping Lightroom for the less involved ones.

    Remote editing and device sharing are made easier with its synchronization with Adobe's cloud services.

5. **Raw Image Support**

    When photographers need to process high-resolution raw photographs and get the greatest quality in their final edits, Lightroom Classic is the program they turn to since it supports a broad range of file formats from numerous camera manufacturers.

6. **Tethered Shooting**

   Studio photographers can take pictures in real time without leaving Lightroom Classic thanks to its tethered shooting capabilities. This facilitates real-time shot monitoring and modifications during filming.

7. **Customizable Presets and Profiles**

   By letting users build or import color profiles and preset, Lightroom Classic streamlines editing operations by making consistent alterations to several photographs at once. These may be customized to fit unique tasks or personal styles.

Differences Between Lightroom and Lightroom Classic

Adobe has two photo editing programs, **Lightroom** (also known as **Lightroom CC**) and **Lightroom Classic**. However, these two versions serve different roles and processes. The main distinctions between them are as follows:

1. **Cloud-Based vs. Desktop-Based**

   Lightroom (Lightroom CC): All your photographs and edits are saved in Adobe's cloud, so you can access them from any device—desktop, mobile, or web—because Lightroom (Lightroom CC) is completely **cloud-based**.

   Lightroom Classic: Photos are saved locally on your computer or external devices and because it is **desktop-based**, Lightroom Classic is perfect for handling huge raw picture collections that don't require internet access.

2. **User Interface and Workflow**

   Lightroom (Lightroom CC): For those new to the program or who are juggling several devices, Lightroom's streamlined interface is a godsend.

   Lightroom Classic: Professional photographers who need sophisticated editing features like tethering and more configurable export choices will find what they need in Lightroom Classic, thanks to its more thorough and feature-rich interface.

3. **Storage and Syncing**

   Lightroom (Lightroom CC): Lightroom facilitates quicker device sync by storing all of your photographs and modifications in the cloud, while it does not offer extensive offline capability.

   Lightroom Classic: Lightroom Classic prioritizes local storage, providing users greater command over the location and method of image backup.

4. **Performance**

   Lightroom (Lightroom CC): Lightroom is designed to be fast when it comes to synchronizing and being accessible on many devices. It's perfect for people who want to make rapid alterations.

   Lightroom Classic: Although it often necessitates a more robust computer, Lightroom Classic is fine-tuned for use with bigger picture collections and high-resolution photos.

Who Should Use Lightroom Classic vs. Lightroom?

Use Lightroom if:

- You desire the flexibility to access your images from any device and appreciate the ease of cloud storage.
- If you use a tablet or mobile phone for editing often, you should be able to sync your work across all of your devices.
- You would rather have an easier-to-navigate UI.

Use Lightroom Classic if:

- You use huge raw picture files and need advanced editing tools since you're a professional or serious photographer.

- You want a greater say over how your picture collection is structured and would rather keep images locally.
- You depend on capabilities such as tethering, personalized printing, or making extensive picture libraries.

CHAPTER 2

MASTERING THE LIGHTROOM CLASSIC INTERFACE

The Lightroom Workspace

There are seven main panels in Lightroom Classic, which makes it an easy-to-use program for editing photos.

Platform Differences:

- **macOS:** The menu bar is at the top of the screen.
- **Windows:** On Windows, the menu bar is below the title bar.

Despite these minor distinctions, the overall design and functionality are the same on Windows and macOS. This ensures a seamless experience for users of both operating systems.

A. Library Filter bar **B.** Image display area **C.** Identity plate **D.** Panels for working with source photos **E.** Filmstrip **F.** Module Picker **G.** Panels for working with metadata, keywords, and adjusting images **H.** Toolbar

Top Panel

The Module Picker is located on the right side of the top panel, while the identity plate is on the left side. Put your company's name or logo on this personalized license plate. Lightroom temporarily displays a progress bar in its stead when background activities are running. A menu item showing Lightroom's current activity will display when you click on the progress bar.

The Module Picker is located on the right side of the screen, and you may navigate between modules by clicking on their titles. The currently used module's name is always highlighted in the Module Picker. When you launch any Lightroom module, you'll get a set of helpful hints. You can navigate the region and get more done with these pointers. To dismiss the hints, click the Close button. To enable the module tips again, go to the Help menu and choose [Module name] Tips.

The Work Area

Most of your time in Lightroom will be spent in the main viewing and work area. While you work, you can choose, assess, organize, compare, edit, and preview your images all from one website. As you go between sections, this main window adapts to display different types of content, such as book layouts, web galleries, print designs, and slide displays.

The Toolbar

The Toolbar is located below the work area. Everything from the tools to the settings is module-specific. You have the option to customize the appearance of the Toolbar for each module independently. Viewing modes, text addition, rating, flagging, labeling, and navigation across sample pages are just a few of the numerous tools and functions at your disposal. The Toolbar may be hidden until you need it, or specific settings can be shown or hidden. By using the T key, you can alter the appearance of the Toolbar.

Looking at the Library module's toolbar, features view mode buttons on the left and customizable task-specific controls and tools on the far right. The available options in the menu will alter as you switch views.

A checkbox next to each name in the Select Toolbar Context menu indicates that the tool or feature is visible in the Toolbar. The order of the tools and options in the Toolbar mirrors that of the menu. On the computer and in the buttons, you'll find many of the same options on the toolbar.

The Filmstrip

No matter where you are in your project, you can always access all your images from the Filmstrip. The Filmstrip allows you to swiftly go through a collection of images or switch between sets without returning to the Library module. Select **Show Filmstrip** from the **Window > Panels menu** or press **F6** to bring the Filmstrip to the bottom of the workspace. Managing images in the Filmstrip is quite similar to managing them in the Library module's Grid view. Metadata develop presets, photo rotation, resizing, and removal are all at your fingertips. You can also rate, flag, and name colors.

Similar to the Grid view in the Library module, the images in the Filmstrip are also there. Depending on your search criteria, it may display all images in the library, images from a specific folder or collection, or a restricted selection.

The Side Panels

Whenever you go to a new module, the side panels will update to display the appropriate resources and tools. To assist in illustrating the layout, think of each module as having two panels: one on the left side that lets you navigate, see previews, discover, and pick photos; and one on the right side that lets you edit or change the parameters for the image you've chosen. Typically, the side panels are arranged in this manner. Now, users of Lightroom Classic 2025 aren't limited to only the Develop module; they may now navigate between panel groups in any module.

On a mac, go to the **menu bar** in Lightroom Classic. On Windows, go to the **Edit menu**. To change the interface, go to **Preferences > Interface** and pick either **Swap Only Develop Left and Right Panel Groups** or **Swap Left and Right Panel Groups**. In the Library module, the left panels (Catalog, Folders, Collections, and Publish Services) help you find pictures and put them in order. You can make changes to the picture you've chosen in the right panels, which are Quick Develop, Keywording, Keyword List, Metadata, and Comments.

Within the Develop module, you can choose Develop presets on the left and change their settings on the right. In the Slideshow, Print, and Web modules, you can pick a layout template from the list on the left and change how it looks on the right.

Customizing the Interface

Modules

Lightroom Classic's module design allows each module to have its own set of tools tailored to its own needs. If you want to make contact sheets from a recent picture session and print them off, for instance, you'll find everything you need under the Print module.

It should be noted that not everyone will utilize every module regularly. Indeed, you may find that certain modules are rarely, if ever, required. The Library and Develop modules are where most Lightroom users spend most of their time. These are where key operations like organizing and editing photographs take place.

Interestingly, Lightroom gives you the ability to hide modules you don't use often, so you may streamline your workspace. You can simplify the UI and zero down on the tools that are crucial to your workflow in this way. This customization can make navigating the software more efficient and less cluttered.

To select which modules to display, right-click on the module panel. A menu will appear:

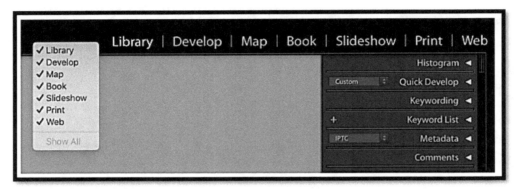

A little checkbox next to the name of each panel in Lightroom Classic allows you to toggle their appearance. To make a module invisible in your workspace, just click on its name in the menu and uncheck the box. That module will then vanish from your workspace.

For example, in my personal Lightroom configuration, I have unchecked the **Book and Slideshow modules** as I do not often use them. This helps to keep my workspace organized. You shouldn't be concerned if you ever require access to a hidden module; they won't be permanently removed. If you look in the Window menu, you can always locate the hidden ones.

You can also access hidden modules quickly by using keyboard shortcuts, which open them when you need them. This will bring the hidden module back to the Module Picker in Lightroom, so keep that in mind. This will cause the module to return to your workspace with the others, so you can quickly find it anytime you need it.

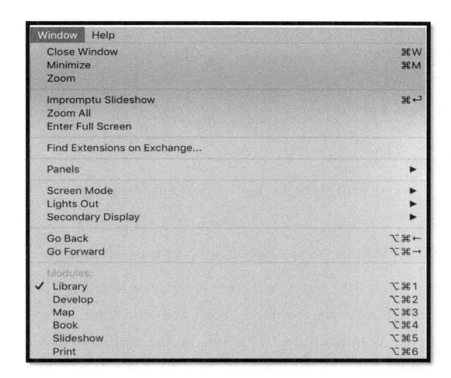

Panels

The following can be seen in the picture above:

A. Library Filter bar

B. Image Display area

C. Identity Plate area

D. Panels displaying photos

E. Filmstrip

F. Module Picker

G. Panels for working with metadata, keywords, adjustments

H. Toolbar

You can customize your workspace to display only the panels that you choose.

Keyboard shortcuts make navigating Lightroom Classic's interface a breeze, and you can use them to control which panels are shown at any one time.

Holding down the **Command key on a Mac or the Ctrl key** on Windows while clicking will open or close all the panels inside a group at once. By toggling all of the panels at once, you may save time compared to altering each one separately.

There is also a fast option to open or close only one panel, which is useful for circumstances like this. Simply hold the **Option key** on a Mac or the **Alt key** on Windows and click on the **panel header**; this will only change the state of that specific panel, the others will remain unchanged.

Both sets of side panels can be seen or hidden at the same time by using the **Tab** key or by navigating to the **Window** menu, selecting **Panel**, and then **Toggle Side Panels**. When you need more room to concentrate on your images without being interrupted by panels on each side, this is a great option.

More so, you can use Shift-Tab to hide any panel in Lightroom, including the side panels, the Module Picker, and the Filmstrip. You can also get the same option by selecting Panels from the Window menu, then Toggle All Panels. When you need to pay your full attention to your photographs, this step will provide you with a workspace free of any distractions.

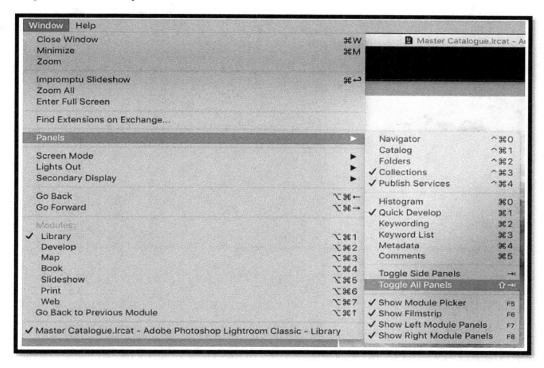

If you don't commonly utilize a certain panel, you can hide it from visibility. To do this, **Control-Click** (Mac) or **Right-Click** (Windows) on any panel header in the group and pick the panel name.

Change the Screen Mode

You can also change how the screen looks to hide the menus, panels, and title bar. Choose **Window**, and then, **Screen Mode**. From the drop-down menu, select an option.

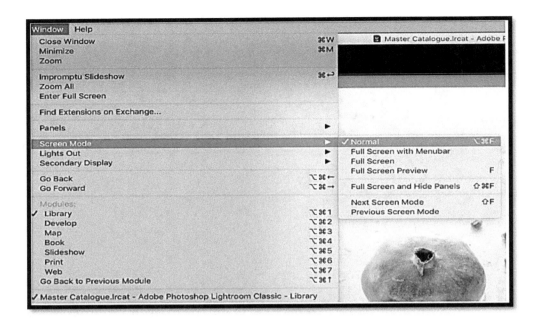

Lightroom Classic makes it easy to switch between multiple viewing modes with the press of a single key. Normal, Full Screen with Menubar and Full Screen are the three primary viewing modes that may be toggled by hitting the F key. You can easily modify your workspace to meet your requirements because of this.

Take care when using macOS's Full Screen and Full Screen with Hide Panels modes. Both of these options will make the Dock hidden, which might also make the application's **Close, Minimize, and Maximize** buttons hidden. In such a case, you can return to these controls by hitting the F key twice; doing so will cycle among the available viewing modes.

While in Full screen mode, you can restore the panels and menu bar by pressing **Shift+Tab** followed by **F**. The panels and menu bar will become visible again, allowing you to quickly access the tools and settings you require.

If you're using a Mac, you can use the shortcut **Command+Option+F,** and if you're using Windows, you can use **Ctrl+Alt+F** to return to the normal screen mode from

Full Screen with Menubar or Full-Screen Mode. You can go back to the standard window view by doing this.

Pressing **Shift+Command+F** on a Mac or **Shift+Ctrl+F** on Windows will bring up a more minimalistic look that hides the title bar, menus, and panels. This ensures that your work area is tidy and uncluttered.

Last but not least, go to **Window > Lights Out** to change the brightness or disable the Lightroom Classic workspace's illumination. By using the F key, you can go through these options and change the lighting to your liking.

Identity Plate

Your photography business's logo can be added to Lightroom using the **Identity Plate Setup.**

You may seem more polished while interacting with customers and using tethered capture with this awesome customization. It will have zero impact on how you carry out your duties.

If you're using Lightroom Classic and want to customize your Identity Plate, here are the steps to do it:

On a Mac, go to the top menu bar and select **Lightroom** to begin. Choose **Identity Plate Setup** from the drop-down menu. On Windows, you'll have to click **Edit** in the top menu and then choose **Identity Plate Setup.**

After you reach the Identity Plate Setup window, navigate to the **Identity Plate** area and search for the **Personalized and Custom** options. Click on this option to begin customizing your Identity Plate.

Just choose **Use a Graphical Identity Plate** and then choose **Locate File**. From there, you can find your picture saved on your computer and choose it to use as your Identity Plate.

Customizing the wording on your ID plate is possible regardless of whether you have a picture or logo to work with. You can make the text seem exactly as you want it to by changing the font, color, and background. Adding a visual element isn't necessary to make your Identity Plate stand out with this customization.

CHAPTER 3

MANAGING THE LIGHTROOM CLASSIC CATALOG
SYSTEM

The catalog file serves as the digital equivalent of a master notebook for all of the photographs in your collection. This digital notebook offers a history of all the modifications you've made, as well as a record of the locations of the master files, any information you added while arranging your photographs, and any other information you created.

The vast majority of individuals will save all of their photographs in a single catalog, which is capable of managing thousands of photographs without running into any issues. Some individuals may wish to create different catalogs for things like their personal images and their business photos. Remember that even though you can create many collections in Lightroom Classic, you can only open one collection at a time. This is a limitation that you must be aware of.

What's in a catalog?

It's something similar to a database, with each of your photographs having its record. This record contains three incredibly significant bits of information on each photograph, and they are as follows:

1. A note about where on your system the picture is
2. Instructions for how you want to process the photo
3. Metadata are things you put on pictures, like ratings and keywords, to help you find or sort them

In the process of adding photographs to Lightroom Classic, a connection is established between the photograph and the catalog record of the photograph. Following that, any modifications that you make to the photograph, such as getting rid of the red eye or adding keywords, are preserved as additional information in the record of the photograph that is stored in the catalog. You can share the photo with others outside of Lightroom Classic by doing things such as printing it, publishing it on Facebook, or creating a slideshow.

If you make any modifications to the metadata, Lightroom Classic will create a duplicate of the photo that includes those modifications. Metadata may be thought of as instructions for developing the picture so that it is accessible to everyone. The photographs that are taken by your camera are not altered in any way by Lightroom Classic. It is possible to modify with Lightroom Classic without causing any damage to the image. You always have the option to return to the original picture that was not altered in any manner.

Lightroom Classic Catalog Versus A File Browser

There is a significant difference between Lightroom Classic and a file reader such as Adobe Bridge. To display files, file browsers need to be able to physically get access to those files. The files must be located on your hard drive or connected to a storage device that contains them for Adobe Bridge to display them to you. There is a catalog that Lightroom Classic uses to keep track of the photographs, which makes this possibility conceivable. Even if the computer is unable to access the picture source files, you will still be able to view a preview of all of the photographs that Lightroom Classic has imported. For example, if Lightroom Classic was used to import files in the past, then the files will still be displayed in the catalog even if they are stored on an external disk. This is the case regardless of whether or not the external drive is connected.

Advantages of the catalog-based workflow

There are two distinct advantages that photographers might obtain from the workflow of the Lightroom Classic library:

1. You can keep your photographs anywhere you choose.

2. Any alterations or updates that you make are nondestructive.

You can save your photographs on the same computer that Lightroom Classic is installed on, on a different hard drive, or even on a drive that is connected to a network. This provides you with more options for managing, editing, and organizing your photographs. When you are working with your photographs with Lightroom Classic, you will be able to observe the modifications you make as you go along since the catalog will preserve a preview of each picture automatically. No changes are made to the source photo files when you use Lightroom Classic.

Best practices for working with Lightroom Classic catalogs

It is important to prepare ahead if you want to produce high-quality work in Lightroom Classic. Putting photographs in more than one catalog, moving catalogs and pictures, combining or merging catalogs, and putting photos in more than one catalog might be difficult to figure out. Furthermore, there is a possibility that the linkages between your catalog and your photographs are broken. The following procedures should be used to plan your catalog configuration to prevent the need to move catalogs and images between computers and disks an excessive number of times.

1. It is important to decide in advance where you will store your Lightroom Classic catalog folder. When it comes to storing it, a network is not the place to do it. It is quite probable that it will be stored on either the hard drive of your computer or an external disk when it is saved. After you have decided where you want to store the list, you should give some thought to the specific folder or path that you want to utilize.

2. Determine where you will save your images going forward. To what extent does your hard disk have available space? Does that suffice? If you use more

than one computer, you might wish to store your photographs and catalog on an external drive that you can connect to any of the computers you use. You should either duplicate the photographs or relocate them to that location before you bring them into Lightroom Classic.

3. Lastly, launch Lightroom Classic and add the photographs to the catalog by positioning them in the same location as they are already located.

Two final recommendations:

- You can possess several Lightroom Classic albums, but you can only utilize a single album at a time. It is possible to have an unlimited number of photographs in a catalog, and Lightroom Classic provides you with a wide variety of options to sort, filter, and organize photographs inside a catalog, as well as to locate them in a short amount of time. Several different items, like tags, labels, groups, folders, and ratings, are available to you. With some careful consideration and experience, you should be able to discover effective methods for managing and organizing all of your photographs within a single catalog.

- If it is necessary, you can relocate or rename photographs while working within Lightroom Classic. Take, for instance, the scenario in which your hard drive becomes full and you need to switch to an external drive; you can do these actions from within Lightroom Classic. People who use Windows or Mac OS X should avoid using Explorer or Finder to relocate photographs that they have saved. Whenever you accomplish that, you will most likely receive **the dreadful photos are missing error**, and you will have to link everything once again.

How to set up your catalog

There are three phases involved in the process of setting up your catalog in Adobe Lightroom Classic. These processes are as follows: creating a catalog, importing photographs, and sorting them in folders.

In addition, there is a folder that represents the list that you create when you create it. The folder and catalog both have the same name, but the name of the folder doesn't end in **catalog**. In this case, the catalog file will be called Wedding Photos.lrcat if you name the folder Wedding Photos. Lightroom Classic makes a sample cache file called Wedding Photos Previews.lrdata and puts it in the same folder as the catalog when you add photos to it.

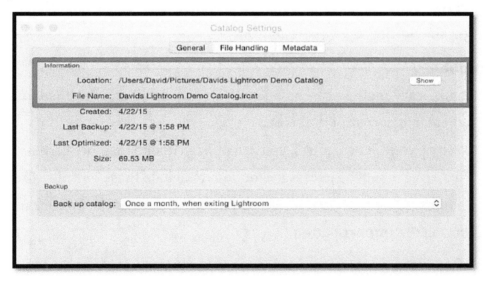

In Lightroom Classic, the program begins from scratch and displays an empty Library module that is prepared for you to add photographs.

Follow these steps in order:

- To begin, launch Adobe Lightroom Classic and proceed to set it up as the initial step. Make sure that the classic version of Adobe Lightroom is successfully installed on your computer by checking the system.

- To access the File menu within the Library module, select it from the list of available options.

- Ensure you select the option labeled **New Catalog**.

- To store the catalog files, select the location on your computer where you wish to save them before proceeding.

- Select a name for your collection that has a significant meaning.

- It will be necessary for you to select the words that will be used for your catalog, including the description of the previews and the metadata settings.

- You can modify these elements according to the settings that you have established for your procedure.

- When you have finished making modifications to the settings that you prefer, you should click the **Create** button.

Import photos

- The Library module can be opened by clicking on it, which is located in the upper right corner of the screen.

- To store your photographs, you can utilize either a memory card or a portable hard drive. It will be necessary for you to include these on your computer.

- To import files, navigate to the bottom left corner of the Library module and click on the **Import** button.

- Please choose the source from which the photographs were obtained. You can pick your camera, an additional hard disk, or something else entirely.
- Decide on the location where the photographs will be copied, the naming of the photographs, and the arrangement of the metadata.
- There is a requirement for you to click on the **Import** button to include the images in your catalog.

Organize your Catalog

- Within the Library module, you can expeditiously render your photographs searchable by giving them the appropriate keywords.
- Make use of collections to organize photographs that go together. Navigate to the Collections panel and then click on the **plus symbol ('+')** to create a new collection.

- To facilitate the process of finding items, it is advisable to provide each photo with information, such as a title, a caption, or a rating.

- Make a circle and assign a star rating to the photographs that you consider to be your finest. Using this, you will be able to select your favorites.

Open a Catalog

When you open a different catalog, Lightroom Classic will start up again and dismiss the catalog that you are currently working with.

1. Select **File** and then **Open Catalog**.
2. In the Open Catalog dialog box, choose the catalog file you want to open, and then click the Open button.

   You also have the option to select a catalog by going to the **File** > **Open Recent tab**.

3. To quit the current catalog and open Lightroom Classic once more, click the **Relaunch** button if you are prompted to do so.

How to upgrade a catalog from a previous version

It is possible to access or import a catalog from an older version of Lightroom Classic, even a beta version if you are using a more recent version of Lightroom Classic. When you do that, Lightroom Classic will make it better than it was before. A new catalog that has been updated has all of the information that was previously included in the old catalog, including images.

1. You should either perform one of the following actions:

   Open Lightroom Classic for the first time.

   Please proceed to the File menu and select Open Catalog if you have already started Lightroom Classic.

2. To open the old catalog, locate **the.lrcat** file and then click the **Open** button. **Note:** If you are unable to recall the location of the old catalog, you can locate it by searching for **lrcat** in either the Explorer (Windows) or the Finder (Mac OS).

3. If you are prompted to do so, select **Relaunch** to close the existing catalog and begin Lightroom Classic from the beginning.

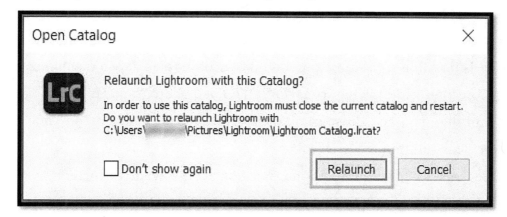

4. Should you so want, you can alter the name of the updated catalog within the Lightroom Catalog Upgrade dialog box. As shown, the name of the catalog will be <currentCatalogName>-v11.

5. Click the **Upgrade** button.

Lightroom Classic Catalog Upgrade

Your catalog will be upgraded in order to access the latest changes in this newer version of Lightroom Classic.

During the upgrade, a copy of your current catalog will be created in the destination indicated below and your old catalog file (.lrcat) will remain intact. Your previews will also be moved to this location and converted for use.

Current Catalog:	Lightroom Catalog.lrcat
Upgraded Catalog:	Lightroom Catalog-v11 .lrcat
Upgraded Catalog File:	/Users, /Documents/Lightroom Catalog-v11.lrcat

Please note: The upgraded catalog will not be compatible with previous versions of Lightroom Classic.

Learn More

Quit   Choose a Different Catalog   Upgrade

Exporting and Deleting a catalog

Export a catalog

Through the process of selecting the photographs and exporting them as a separate catalog, it is possible to create a catalog that encompasses only a portion of a larger catalog. Consider the following scenario: you upload photographs to a catalog on your laptop, and then you add those same pictures to a master catalog on your desktop computer. This solution is beneficial.

1. Please select the photographs that you would want to include in the new catalog.

2. Go to the **File** menu, and select **Export As Catalog.**

3. Please specify the name of the catalog as well as its location.

4. Click the **Save button** (Windows) or the **Export Catalogue** button (Mac OS) once you have decided if you want to export the previews and negative files (Mac OS).

    The **negative files** were the very first files that were imported into Lightroom Classic.

34

The newly updated catalog includes information on the selected photographs as well as links to those pictures. You will need to open the catalog to view the new one.

5.   You have the option of importing a new catalog into an existing one if you wish to join two or more catalogs together.

Delete a catalog

The deletion of a catalog will result in the loss of all of the work that you have completed in Lightroom Classic that has not been preserved in the photo files. Even though the previews have been removed, the source photographs to which they link are still accessible.

- Find the folder that contains your catalog in Explorer (Windows) or Finder (Mac OS), and then drag it to the Trash (Mac OS) or Recycling Bin (Windows) to proceed with the process.

  Be sure that the folder you intend to remove has only the catalog files you want to get rid of, and that it does not contain any other files.

To expedite the process, Lightroom Classic will add a Previews folder to the Explorer (Windows) or Finder (Mac OS) window that is located next to the .lrcat file. Provided that the name of this folder is identical to the name of the .lrcat file, it is OK to delete this folder. If you delete a Previews folder that will still be required by a catalog, Lightroom Classic will recreate it whenever you operate within that specified catalog. On the other hand, until the previews are rebuilt, it will take more time to become operational.

Moving catalogs to a new location

Before you move or copy the files, it is important to make a copy of the catalog and the sample files.

1. Find the folder containing the preview and catalog files. For Windows, go to **Edit > Catalog Settings in Lightroom Classic**. For Mac OS X, go to **Lightroom Classic > Catalog Settings.**

2. It is possible to open the catalog in Windows Explorer or Mac OS X Finder by clicking the Show button located in the Information section of the General panel.

3. Quit Lightroom Classic.

4. The catalog.lrcat, catalog.lrcat-data, Previews.lrdata, and (if it is available) Smart Previews.lrdata files should be copied or moved to the new place in Explorer (Windows) or Finder (Mac OS).

5. Simply double-click **on the .lrcat** file that has been moved to its new location to access it in Lightroom Classic.

6. If you choose to, Lightroom Classic will display an icon that looks like a question mark next to the names of folders in the Folders panel and an icon that looks like an exclamation point next to image thumbnails in the Grid view if it is unable to locate folders or photographs in the catalog that has been duplicated or moved. You can retrieve the folder links by right-clicking (on Windows) or Control-clicking (on Mac OS) on a folder that has the appearance of a question mark and selecting **Find Missing Folder.**

Change the default catalog

When Lightroom Classic is started up, it automatically opens the most recent library that has been created. You can alter this behavior so that it opens a different store or always prompts you to choose one.

1. Simply navigate to **Edit > Preferences** on Windows. **Lightroom Classic > Preferences** is the menu option to select on Mac OS X.

2. One of the following options can be selected from the When Starting Up Use This Catalog menu, which can be found in the General tab:

Load Most Recent Catalog

Opens the most recent list that you were working with at the time.

Prompt Me When Starting Lightroom

You will be able to decide on the **Select Catalog** dialog box has been shown.

A catalog in the default location

You can select from all the catalogs in \Pictures\Lightroom (Windows) or /Pictures/Lightroom (Mac OS) listed by Lightroom Classic.

Other

You can go to a certain catalog file (.lrcat) and select it as the one that should open automatically when the application is started.

Customize catalog settings

Within the Catalog Settings dialog box, you can instruct Lightroom Classic collections in a variety of ways regarding how you would like them to behave.

1. Select **Edit** > **Catalog Settings** from the menu bar in Windows. **Lightroom Classic** > **Catalog Settings** is the menu option to select in Mac OS X.

2. Within the General tab, select any one of the following options:

   Information

   The position, filename, and creation date of the catalog are some of the information that is provided by this service. Simply click the Show button to view the catalog file in either the Windows Explorer or the Mac OS Finder.

   Backup

   Using this option, you can select the frequency with which the current catalog is backed up.

3. Make your selection from the following options inside the File Handling tab:

Preview Cache

Specifies how Lightroom Classic presents the three different kinds of image previews. The preview cache file, located in the folder that contains your catalog, is where all of the previews store themselves.

Standard Preview Size

Specifies the maximum length, in pixels, of the long side of full-size rendered previews. Choose a size that is either the same as or larger than the actual quality of the screen you are using. If the dimensions of your screen are 1920 by 1200 pixels, for instance, select the Standard Preview Size > 2048 Pixels option. On the other hand, if the size of your screen is more than 2048 pixels, Lightroom Classic will generate a 1:1 preview instead.

Preview Quality

Sets the appearance of the thumbnail pictures to be shown. The JPEG quality scale is comparable to the levels of quality, which are high, medium, and low respectively.

Automatically Discard 1:1 Previews

The application is informed by this option when it is appropriate to discard 1:1 previews, which is determined by the most recent access to the preview. You can observe how the sharpening and noise reduction processes are carried out when you look at a 1:1 preview, which means that the pixels are the same size as the original photographs. If you leave them around for an excessive amount of time, the catalog preview file may become rather large. They are created on an as-needed basis.

Smart Previews

The amount of space that Smart Previews is using up on the disk is displayed here.

Import Sequence Numbers

This function allows you to set the initial sequence numbers for any photographs that you add to the library. The Import Number is the first number in a sequence that provides information about the number of import activities that have been completed. There is a series of numbers that indicate the total number of photographs that have been uploaded to the catalog. The first of these numbers is the number of Photos Imported.

4. Make your selection from the following choices on the Metadata tab:

Offer Suggestions From Recently Entered Values

Although you are typing a metadata item that appears to be one that you have already typed, one or more ideas will appear as you type. Please uncheck this option to turn it off. To remove outdated items, select the **Clear All Suggestion Lists option**.

Include Develop Settings In Metadata Inside JPEG, TIFF, PNG, And PSD Files

Lightroom Classic will not add the settings for the Develop module to the XMP metadata of JPEG, TIFF, PNG, and PSD files if you choose this choice. These include the settings for the Develop module.

Automatically Write Changes Into XMP

If you select this option, any modifications that you make to the metadata will be stored straight in the XMP sidecar files. When this occurs, other applications will be able to observe these modifications. Make sure that this option is not checked if you just want to save changes to the metadata in the catalog.

Enable Reverse Geocoding of GPS Coordinates To Provide Address Suggestions

dditionally, if the GPS coordinates of your photos are accessible, Lightroom Classic can upload them to Google. This enables Lightroom Classic to determine the city, state, and nation of the photograph, and then add that information to the metadata associated with the IPTC Location element.

Export Reverse Geocoding Suggestions Whenever Address Fields Are Empty

If you select this option, Lightroom Classic will include your exported photographs with the IPTC Location metadata that is advised by Google.

Write Date Or Time Changes Into Proprietary Raw Files

When you make a change to the metadata of a photograph's capture time (Metadata > Edit Capture Time), this feature gives you the ability to select whether or not Lightroom Classic will add a new date and time to proprietary raw files. This option is not selected automatically by default.

Optimize the catalog

Following the addition, modification, or deletion of a large number of files, Lightroom Classic may become less responsive. If this occurs, you should optimize your catalog to make it operate more quickly.

Choose **File > Optimize Catalog** on your menu.

Plan your backup strategy

You have the option of configuring Lightroom Classic to create a backup of your catalog each time you exit the software. In Lightroom Classic, the catalog file is the only one that is preserved when you do a backup. Your modified photographs and everything else that you transmit from Lightroom Classic needs to be backed up on your own for your protection.

The compilation of backups of the catalog regularly is just one component of what ought to be a comprehensive backup strategy. During the process of developing a backup plan:

It is important to keep in mind that the more often you back up your catalog and images, the less chance you have to lose data if something goes wrong.

Your backup copies of your photographs and documents should be stored on a hard drive that is not linked to the one that contains your work files. This will ensure that your backups are safe and secure.

To manage the process and ensure that both your working files and your backup files are always up to date with any changes, you might wish to make use of backup software.

If you are concerned about the possibility of accidentally erasing your backup data, you should create additional copies on various CDs or media that cannot be read, such as DVDs.

Always store your backup disk in a separate location from your working disk, preferably outside of the house or in a safe that is resistant to fire. This will ensure that your data remains secure.

You may wish to create duplicates of your photographs once you have imported them. It is important to keep in mind that this just replicates the original photographs and not the changes that you have made to them.

It is the default behavior of Lightroom Classic to save backed-up collections in the following locations:

Windows: \Users\[user name]\Pictures\Lightroom\[catalog name]\Backups\

Mac OS: /Users/[user name]/Pictures/Lightroom/[catalog name]/Backups\

Lightroom Classic creates a folder under the Backups folder that contains the date and time of the backup in the format of **YYYY-MM-DD HRMN**. On a 24-hour clock, there is no gap between the hours and minutes to indicate the time. The backed-up catalog is stored in a folder that has a date stamp on it, and it has the same name as the catalog that is present. When Lightroom Classic creates a backup, it additionally creates a new catalog for the backup. To free up space on your hard disk, you should either delete outdated backup files or reduce their size. In addition to this, you need to make sure that you can write to the folder that you intend to keep your backup in.

Schedule catalog backups

1. Select **Edit** > **Catalog Settings** from the menu bar in Windows. **Lightroom Classic** > **Catalog Settings** is the menu option to select in Mac OS X.

2. From the menu that displays in the Back-Up section of the General panel, select one of the following selections:

When Lightroom Next Exits

On the subsequent occasion that you close Lightroom Classic, a backup of the catalog is created. The option to **Back Up Catalog** will then be changed to **Never** after that.

Every Time Lightroom Exits

Lightroom Classic creates a backup of the catalog each time you close the program, ensuring that any changes you make are always preserved.

Once A Day, When Exiting Lightroom

The catalog is backed up every day when you close Lightroom Classic for the first time; this happens continuously. It is not possible to make any modifications to Lightroom Classic once you have left it for longer than one day. There will be no saving of the modifications until the next day.

Once A Week, When Exiting Lightroom

There is a copy of the catalog that is saved once per week. If you close Lightroom Classic more frequently, more modifications will not be stored until the next week arrives.

Once A Month, When Exiting Lightroom

It saves a copy of the catalog once every month. If you close Lightroom Classic more frequently, additional modifications will not be stored until the following month.

Never

There are no saves that can be made using Lightroom Classic. (Not Recommended.)

Back up a catalog automatically

1. Close Lightroom Classic once you have completed the process of creating a backup for your catalog in the Catalog Settings.

2. The catalog can be backed up to the default location by clicking the **Back Up** button in the **Back Up Catalog** dialog box when prompted to do so. Then, lightroom classic should be closed.

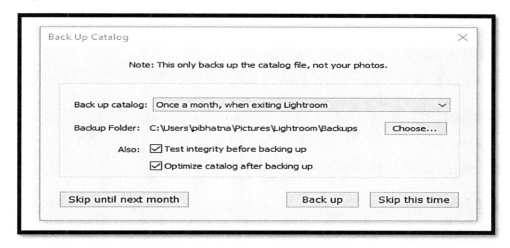

Before clicking the Back Up button, you have the option of selecting any of the following options:

Backup Folder

This displays the location inside Lightroom Classic where files are saved by default. Click the Choose button to back up to a different location.

Test Integrity Before Backing Up

Before Lightroom Classic finishes backing up, you should check to determine if the catalog has been corrupted. As a result of testing the catalog's integrity, the process of backing it up takes more time, but the likelihood of losing data is reduced.

Note: If you open a catalog, you will also have the opportunity to verify if it is accurate. Select **When Starting Up Use This Catalog** from the General panel of the Preferences dialog box, and then select **Prompt Me When Starting Lightroom** with the appropriate option. Next, launch Lightroom Classic on your computer. In the Select Catalog dialog box, pick the option to **Test Integrity of This Catalog**, and then click the **Open** button.

Optimize Catalog After Backing Up

It will clean up and restructure your database file to make it function more efficiently and effectively.

Skip Until Tomorrow

If you select to back up your catalog every day, click to put it off for one more day.

Skip Until Next Week

The option to take a week off from backing up your catalog is available to you if you have chosen to do so once every week.

Skip Until Next Month

Click this button to postpone the backup of your catalog for one month if you have decided to back it up once a month.

Skip This Time

After clicking, you will be able to postpone the saving process until the next time you close Lightroom Classic.

Back up a catalog manually

1. Select **Edit > Catalog Settings** from the menu bar in Windows. **Lightroom Classic > Catalog Settings** is the menu option to select in Mac OS X.
2. **Back-Up Catalog** should be selected, followed by **When Lightroom Next Exits**.

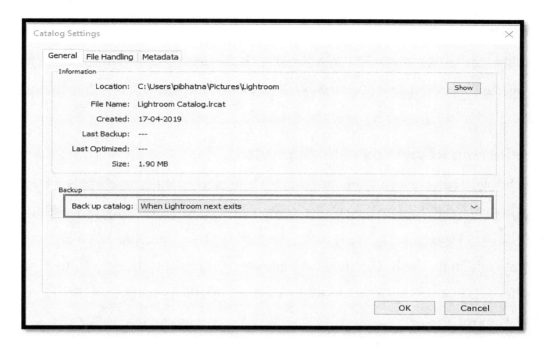

3. It is recommended that Lightroom Classic be closed after the window has been closed.

Restore a backup catalog

1. The backup file should be located and opened.
2. Make sure to select **File** and then **Open Catalog**.
3. Discover the location where you stored the copy of the catalog file that you created.
4. Following the selection of the .lrcat and .lrcat-data files that you backed up, click the **Open** button.
5. You can update the original catalog by copying the backed-up catalog to the location where the original catalog is kept. This step is optional.

Copying keywords to a new catalog

You could just create keywords from scratch; however, there is a possibility that the spelling, capitalization, and hierarchy will be incorrect. This will result in duplication and more labor when you connect the catalog.

Transferring keywords using a photo

To do this, you can select one image from your primary catalog and apply every term that you have on that image. Going to the **Metadata menu** and selecting **Save Metadata to File**, you can save the keywords. After that, the keywords will be automatically included in the new catalog when you upload the photo to it. On the other hand, if you do this a lot, it will be easy to overlook changes to the list of your primary keywords.

Transferring keywords using Export Keywords

It's better to extract just the keywords. To do this:

1. From the Metadata window, choose the **Export Keywords** option. It's possible to export to either an Include Keyword Tag Options (.csv file) or an Exclude Keyword Tag Options (.txt file) file. Both of them will be organized in the same manner as your primary catalog. Your Export settings are included in the.csv file (with Tags) if terms are included in the Export category. Aside from that, they are just as effective as one another.

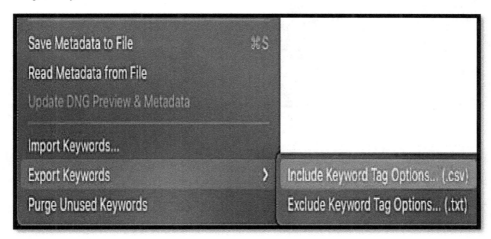

2. Please store this in a temporary location. There are tabs in the text file that display the hierarchy, just as in the image that can be found below (on the left). Some tabs have been maintained in the Keyword name entry of the right csv file, which gives the impression that it is the correct one.

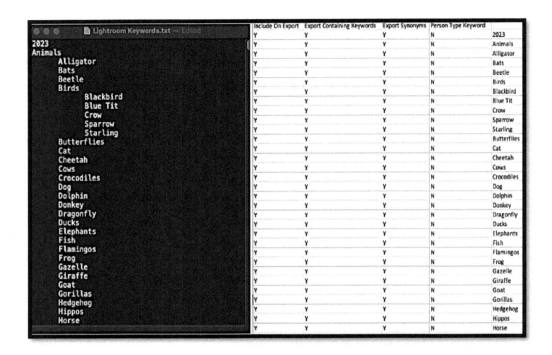

Include On Export	Export Containing Keywords	Export Synonyms	Person Type Keyword	
Y	Y	Y	N	2023
Y	Y	Y	N	Animals
Y	Y	Y	N	Alligator
Y	Y	Y	N	Bats
Y	Y	Y	N	Beetle
Y	Y	Y	N	Birds
Y	Y	Y	N	Blackbird
Y	Y	Y	N	Blue Tit
Y	Y	Y	N	Crow
Y	Y	Y	N	Sparrow
Y	Y	Y	N	Starling
Y	Y	Y	N	Butterflies
Y	Y	Y	N	Cat
Y	Y	Y	N	Cheetah
Y	Y	Y	N	Cows
Y	Y	Y	N	Crocodiles
Y	Y	Y	N	Dog
Y	Y	Y	N	Dolphin
Y	Y	Y	N	Donkey
Y	Y	Y	N	Dragonfly
Y	Y	Y	N	Ducks
Y	Y	Y	N	Elephants
Y	Y	Y	N	Fish
Y	Y	Y	N	Flamingos
Y	Y	Y	N	Frog
Y	Y	Y	N	Gazelle
Y	Y	Y	N	Giraffe
Y	Y	Y	N	Goat
Y	Y	Y	N	Gorillas
Y	Y	Y	N	Hedgehog
Y	Y	Y	N	Hippos
Y	Y	Y	N	Horse

3.   Open your new catalog, navigate to the Metadata menu, choose import keywords, and then select the Lightroom Keywords.txt file that you created. This will allow you to accomplish the import of keywords.

At long last, you have it! Going to the Keywords panel will allow you to view all of your keywords as well as the order in which they are listed in your primary catalog.

Nevertheless, it is important to keep in mind that it does not automatically update itself if you alter the list of keywords in your primary catalog.

CHAPTER 4

NAVIGATING THE LIBRARY MODULE

Importing and Organizing Photos

The process of adding your photographs to Lightroom Classic may be done in several different ways. It is possible to bring them in immediately from a digital camera or card reader, as well as from your hard disk or any other external storage device. Additionally, it is possible to transfer them from one Lightroom catalog to another or from another application. The process of importing is simple; all you need to do is click a button or use a command from the file menu. After you have connected your camera, Lightroom will begin the process of importing the images. Additionally, it can import immediately once you move files into a particular location. The Import dialog box is a tool that you should become familiar with, regardless of the source from which you obtain your photographs.

The first few phases of the import process are displayed in the upper half of the Import dialog box, running from left to right. These processes include selecting an import source, instructing Lightroom on how to handle the files that you are importing, and then, if you wish to copy or transfer the source files, setting up an import location. It is possible to leave the dialog box in compact mode if you are already familiar with these things and it is still your intention to load the photographs. If you want to see even more information, you may expand the dialog box by clicking the arrow in the bottom left corner of the screen.

When the dialog box is enlarged, it appears and functions in a manner that is similar to that of the workspace sections in Lightroom Classic. You can access any disk that contains your data by using the Source box, which is located on the left. When using either the Grid view or the Loupe view, the Preview area located in the middle displays thumbnails of images taken from the source. There is a possibility that the right panel group has a Destination panel that exhibits the same appearance as the Source panel. Additionally, there is a possibility that there are controls for editing your photographs while they are being imported.

Importing photos from a digital camera

The majority of the instructions for importing from a camera are provided in this section; however, you should first test it out with a few of your photographs. You are free to print off ten to fifteen photographs of anything you choose. All that is required of you is to have anything on the memory card that you can utilize throughout the process of importing.

When you initially attach your camera or memory card to your computer, the first thing you need to do is make sure that Lightroom is configured in such a way that the process of importing begins immediately.

1. Navigate to **Lightroom Classic > Preferences** on your macOS device. Go to **Edit > Preferences** on your Windows computer. Within the Preferences dialog box, click on the **General tab**. In the Import Options section, check the box next to the option that says **Show Import Dialog When A Memory Card Is Detected**.

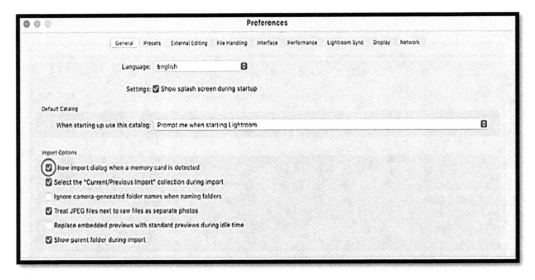

Names are assigned to the folders on the memory card by certain cameras. Consider using the option to **Ignore Camera-Generated Folder Names**

When Naming Folders if you do not like the names of these folders and would like to arrange your photographs more effectively.

2. For the Preferences dialog box to be closed, either click the **Close** or **OK** button.

3. To connect your digital camera or card reader to your computer, you will need to follow the instructions that originally came with it.

4. This step may be different for you if you have image management tools installed on your computer or if you use a different operating system:

    o   If the AutoPlay dialog box or options pane appears in Windows, select the option to open image files in Lightroom Classic. Changing this to the default setting may be accomplished by heading to the Start menu and selecting **Settings > Devices > AutoPlay.**

    o   If the Adobe Downloader dialog box appears on your computer and you already own another Adobe image management application, such as Adobe Bridge, promptly click the **Cancel** button.

    o   You should proceed to step 5 if the Import dialog box appears.

    o   If the Import dialog box fails to appear, you may either click the **Import** button located beneath the group on the left panel or navigate to the **File** menu and select **Import Photos and Video.**

5. When the Import dialog box appears in compact mode, you may view all of the options that are available in the larger Import dialog box by clicking the **Show More options** button that is located in the bottom left corner of the dialog box.

The process of importing consists of three phases, which are displayed on the top panel of the Import dialog box, which may be seen in both the tiny and big formats. These steps are listed chronologically from left to right.

- Select the location from which the photographs you wish to incorporate into your catalog originated.
- Providing Lightroom with instructions on how to manage the files that you are importing.
- There is the process of establishing the place where the photo files will be copied. You can select any develop presets, keywords, or other information that you wish to apply to your photographs while they are being uploaded to your collection. This decision is made below this panel.

Your camera or memory card is now displayed as the source to import from in the FROM section on the left side of the top panel and under Devices in the Source section on the left side of the Import dialog box. Both of these sections are located on the left side of the top panel.

The configuration of your computer determines whether or not it will recognize the memory card attached to your camera as a portable storage drive. If this is the case, the options that are available in the Import dialog box could be altered; nevertheless, this should not affect anything else.

NOTE: Please take note that if your memory card is seen as a detachable disk, it is possible that the Move and Add options will not be disabled.

6.   Assuming that your memory card is displayed in the Source panel as a removable disk rather than a device, you will need to select it by clicking on it in the Files list, and then you will need to ensure that the Include Subfolders checkbox is selected.

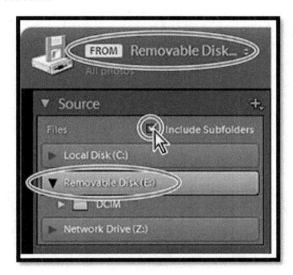

7.   To copy the photographs from your camera onto your hard drive, select Copy from the import type drop-down menu in the middle of the top panel to copy the photos from your camera to your hard drive. Your catalog will then be updated with the photographs, but the original files will continue to be stored on the memory card that is included within your camera.

Lightroom displays a brief explanation of what will take place along with each option that is now selected.

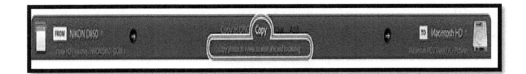

8. A tooltip will show whenever you move your cursor over one of the options in the bar that spans the top of the Preview window. This tooltip will provide you with further information on that particular option. It is not yet time to click the Import button; instead, keep the All Photos option in its current state.

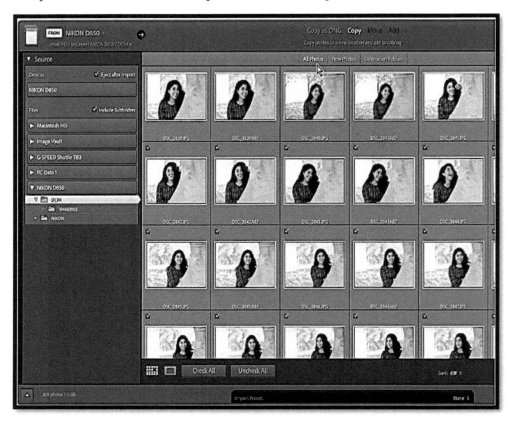

An image will be imported into the program if there is a checkmark in the upper left corner of the image cell. By default, every one of the photographs stored on your memory card will be selected to be imported. You can deselect a photo by clicking on its checkbox should you decide that you do not wish to download it.

TIP: You can adjust the size of the thumbnails by dragging the slider that is located below the right side of the preview pane.

You can choose several pictures and make changes to all of their checkmarks for all of them at the same time. To create a collection of images that are compatible with one another, first click on the thumbnail or the image cell that surrounds the first image in the group. Next, while holding down the Shift key, click on the image that is the final one in the collection. To choose specific photographs, you can either Command-click or Ctrl-click on their icons. Changing the import status of any photo for the entire group can be accomplished by clicking the checkbox located next to the picture.

You can see that the Copy option is selected rather than the Add option at the very top of the import window. During the process of importing, it is important to keep in mind that Lightroom does not import the various photo files, rather, it involves adding entries to the Lightroom catalog to display the locations of the files. Because you are moving the files, you will be required to select a location.

If you select **Add**, rather than **Copy**, you would not be required to select a folder to transmit the photographs. They would remain in the location where they have previously been preserved. However, because memory cards are designed to be removed and used again, you should not have your photographs stored on them for an indefinite period. Lightroom does not provide you with the Add and Move options when you import from a camera because it believes that you will copy your photographs from the memory card to a more permanent location.

As a result, the following step is to select a folder in which your photographs should be copied. Now is the time to seriously consider how you would like to organize the photographs that are stored on your hard disk.

Importing photos from a folder on a hard drive

In the process of adding photographs to Lightroom Classic, a connection is established between the photograph and the catalog record of the photograph.

During the import process, the window for the import operates from left to right. To begin, locate the files that you wish to import (the source files) on the left side of the screen. The next step is to select whether you want to add, move, or copy them to the catalog where they are located in the middle of the window. In conclusion, you can select the target folder for the files as well as additional parameters for the imported files on the right side of the screen.

Note: Remember that before you begin the process of importing images for the first time, you should first consider how you want to organize them and where you will keep them. It is possible that you may not have to move photographs as frequently if you plan, which will make it easier for you to keep track of them in your catalog.

1.   Perform one of the following actions to access the import window:
     o   Locate the Import button in the Library module, which is located in the bottom left corner, and then click on it.
     o   To import photos and videos, navigate to the main menu and pick **File > Import Photos and Video.**
     o   In the Windows version of Explorer or the Mac OS version of Finder, you can drag a folder or individual files into the Grid view. Skip Step 2 after this.

A. Preview area **B.** Source panel **C.** Toggle Minimal import **D.** Options and Destination panels

2. Choose the Source panel, which is located on the left side of the import window, or click the **Select A Source or From** button, which is located in the top left corner of the window. By doing so, you will be able to locate the files that you wish to import.

   Note: Take note that the Source panel displays networks that are connected. To add a network location, click From or Select A Source, pick Other Source, and then find the folder that is connected to the network. Click the plus sign (+) that is located next to the name of the Source panel in Windows, and then select the option that says Add Network Volume.

3. To add the images to the catalog, select the method that you wish to use at the top center of the import window, which offers the following options:

Copy As DNG

In addition to converting any raw camera data to the Digital Negative (DNG) format, it transfers the photographed images to the folder that you select.

Copy

Copies the picture files and any extra files to the folder you specify.

Move

Move all of the photo files as well as any sidecar files to the folder that you have chosen. It is removed from the location where the files are currently located.

Add

Keeps the photo files at the location where they are currently in.

4. Browse through the preview area located in the middle of the import window to locate the photographs that you wish to import, and then select them. The photo is selected to be imported, as shown by the presence of a checkmark in the upper left-hand corner of the thumbnail on the screen.

    o   If you want to filter photographs in the preview, you can choose any of the following options:

All Photos

A complete removal of all filters.

New Photos

Excludes photographs that have previously been imported as well as those that are suspected of being duplicates.

Destination Folders

Sort the photographs according to the folder that they are going to be placed in (this feature is only available when transferring or copying photos into a catalog).

The photographs will be displayed in the folders that they will be saved in when you click the Destination Folders, which is located above the preview area. The Destination panel is located on the right side of the screen, and it displays the folders that will be added in bold, as well as the number of photographs that will be stored in those folders.

- To magnify a single image, you may zoom in on it by clicking the **Loupe view button** located on the toolbar.

- You can choose or deselect all of the photographs in the folder at once by clicking on the **Check All** or **Uncheck All** button located in the toolbar.

- If you want to sort photographs according to the time they were shot, whether they are checked, the name of the file, or the kind of media (video or image), you can perform this by clicking the Sort pop-up option that is located in the toolbar.

- Move the images slider to alter the size of the photographs that are displayed in the grid.

- At the upper left corner of a preview, there is a box that you may click to select which photographs you want to display or hide. On the other hand, you can choose or delete photographs by pressing the Alt-click (Windows) or Option-click (Mac OS) button on any section of the picture.

5. If you move or copy the photographs and then import them, you have the option of selecting where to put them. To accomplish this, select a location for the images by clicking **To** located in the upper right-hand corner of the window. On the Destination panel, you can also select alternative possibilities by clicking on a location, such as the following:

Into Subfolder

Transfer the images you've imported to a different folder or make a copy of them. Put the new folder's name into the text box.

Organize

You can organize the pictures in the new subfolder in three ways: keep the folder structure from the original folder, make subfolders based on date, or put all the photos in one folder.

Date Format

Decide on a format for writing the dates.

Note: When you import, new folders will be created in the Destination panel if the folder names are in italics. Inspect the Destination panel carefully to ensure that you are importing the images to the correct location.

6. To modify further settings for the imported files, use the checkboxes on the window's right side.

    When you're ready to add photographs to your Lightroom Classic catalog, choose them from the drop-down menu. After that, you'll see various panels on the right side of the import window where you can customize the photos.

7. Proceed to Import. Click Done to save the changes you made to the import settings even if you don't want to import right now.

Back up photos during import

Before you transfer or copy images into the library, you can create a backup of the original files. Pick **Make A Second Copy To** from the File Handling panel on the right side of the import window and choose a place.

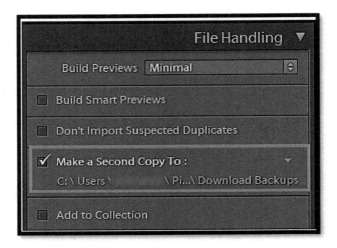

Ignore duplicates when importing

To determine if an image is a duplicate of another in the library, Lightroom Classic compares the original filename, Exif capture time and date, and file size. Lightroom Classic has an option that lets you tell it to not import identical files.

Choose Don't Import Suspected Duplicates from the File Handling box on the right side of the import window.

Specify initial previews

You have the option to display a lower-quality preview of an imported image immediately or a higher-quality preview when Lightroom Classic produces the image.

Since embedded previews are created by cameras and do not have color management, Lightroom Classic does not comprehend them in the same manner as camera raw files. Previews in Lightroom Classic are color-controlled, but require more time to produce.

- Inside the File Handling panel on the import window's right side, you should see the Build Previews menu. Pick one of these options:

Minimal

Use the little previews that are already there to see the photographs straight away. When necessary, Lightroom Classic generates standard-sized previews.

Embedded & Sidecar

Show the camera's largest detectable preview. This option is quicker than creating a standard-size preview, even though it may take more time than a Minimal preview.

Standard

Show previews as they are being made by Lightroom Classic. At the Fit Zoom level of the Loupe view, you can observe samples of standard size. For color management, they rely on Adobe RGB. The Standard sample size may be found in the Catalog Settings dialog box.

1:1

You should only see previews that display the actual photos in their entirety.

- To generate Smart Previews for the photographs you've stored, select Build Smart Previews.

Smart Previews allows you to edit images independently of your computer. Smart Preview files are compact, lightweight, and based on the lossy DNG format.

Work with Embedded Previews

Select **Build Previews** as **Embedded & Sidecar** from the File Handling menu located in the Import window's upper right corner. This will make embedded previews.

By using this preview option, you can swiftly go through a vast collection of photographs in the Library module and perform 1:1 zoom with ease. The order in which the embedded samples are shown is determined by the folder you are now viewing. For example, you can begin browsing your images immediately after adding them to more than one folder if you import them.

In the Library module, Embedded Previews are indicated by 🔲 icon in the Grid view and *Embedded Preview* overlay text in the Loupe view as shown below.

When viewing images in Grid view, you may find the Embedded Preview icon in the upper left corner of the thumbnail.

The embedded preview overlay text is located in the bottom right corner of the photo in the Loupe view.

Rename photos when importing

Before importing photographs into the catalog, you have the option to select the file names.

1. On the right side of the import window, you should see the Rename Files checkbox. Check the box.

2. The Template box will appear; from there, choose a name option. To use a specific name, choose the option that allows it and then type it into the Custom Text area.

3. To prevent a custom number sequence from starting with 1, you have the option to enter a number in the Start Number field.

Additional FAQ Related to Importing in Lightroom

Where does Lightroom store imported photos?

There is no photo storage in Lightroom. It is limited to syncing with previously imported images. The real images are not moved. Making a Lightroom Catalog is how this is done.

Can folders be imported into Lightroom?

To import the whole folder into Lightroom, you may just drag & drop it into the window. As the images are typically located in the category subfolders, make sure to import everything by checking the box that reads **Include subfolders.**

What happens if I import photographs and then reorganize them in my storage?

If you move an image from its original location, Lightroom will no longer be able to sync with it since it is limited to working with the original files. Afterward, a blank space will be displayed adjacent to the image's thumbnail. Lightroom will then ask you to pick a new location to store the updated image when you right-click on the thumbnail.

Additional Tips

- **Previewing and Selecting**: You can choose which photographs to import and which ones to leave out before the actual import.
- **Presets**: Import presets allow you to store settings for subsequent usage, which speeds up your work.
- **Backup**: While the import is running, you might consider creating a secondary location for backups. The **Make a Second Copy to** option, which is situated beneath the **Destination** choice, allows you to accomplish this.

CHAPTER 5

ARRANGING PHOTOS WITH FOLDERS AND COLLECTIONS

A restaurant's extensive menu might be bewildering, if you're anything like me. Having a limited menu makes it much easier to choose what to eat.

The same goes for pictures.

When you can see a small collection of images at a glance it's easier to cherry-pick the ones you want.

Rather than Folders, Lightroom Collections are the key here. Instead of browsing through each photo in a folder, you can see a bunch of them in a collection.

But that's not all.

There are four distinct kinds of collections in Lightroom, and each one serves a specific purpose.

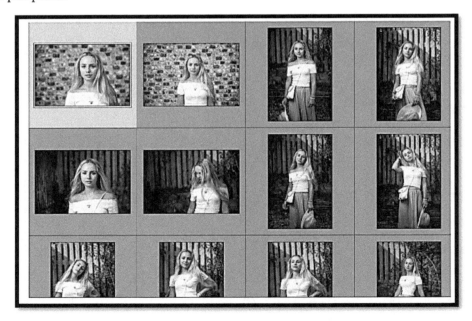

What's the difference between Folders and Collections in Lightroom?

Lightroom Folders

- The Library module is the sole way to access the folders where your images are stored.
- You can see the structure of your file system in the folders. Photos on your computer are kept there. The computer will replicate your actions when you move or delete folders.
- There is a limit of one folder per photo.

Lightroom Collections

- When you create a virtual copy of a photo in a Collection within Lightroom, this virtual copy will also appear in the Folder where the original photo is stored. This implies that the virtual copies are still associated with their original locations, even if the Collection is a temporary place to organize and display your images.

- Collections are accessible and manageable from any Lightroom module, giving you a lot of flexibility in organizing your photographs without the hassle of deleting them. You can temporarily save your photographs in collections, which provides you the ability to group and browse them as needed.

- The original file will be kept in the Folder even after deleting a photo from a Collection. You have to remove the photo from the folder as well as Lightroom for it to be fully deleted. This could be annoying if you often make virtual copies of images so you can see how various versions of the same file look. If you aren't cautious, you can easily get more than one copy of the same picture.

- Clear out the Collection and the Folder of any unnecessary photographs to maintain a neat catalog. Your library will get inundated with duplicate photographs if you don't.

- The images and folders included inside a Collection will remain unaffected when the Collection is removed. No changes are made to the files or their locations while using collections; they are only tools for organization.

It is possible to combine images from several distinct folders into a single collection. You can find the same photo in many collections, but it will only ever display in one folder.

Before you get to the book module to design your book, it's a good idea to put photos for your photo book into collections. This will help you focus on your options.

Kinds of Lightroom collections

There are four types of Lightroom collections:

1. Collections

2. Quick Collections

3. Target Collections

4. Smart Collections

1. Collections

These are collections that you create and populate manually.

How Collections work

Viewing a set of images from a shoot is the most common use case for these Lightroom collections. The fact that the Develop module provides access to Collections, as opposed to Folders, makes them quite helpful.

To create a Collection:

- Click the + symbol next to collections.

- Pick **Create Collection** from the menu option that appears.

- Name your collection and check or uncheck the Include selected photos box.

- You can add it to a Collection Set by checking the box and then choosing the Collection Set.

▼ Catalog	
All Photographs	3752
All Synced Photographs	0
Quick Collection +	26
Previous Import	737
Previous Export as Catalog	1281

2.   **Quick Collections**

By pressing the B key or selecting Add to Quick Collection from the context menu after right-clicking the mouse button, you can add photographs to this Lightroom collection.

In a nutshell, Quick Collections are perfect for building temporary collections fast.

How Quick Collections work

The first thing I do when I sit down to write an article for Lounge is compile a Quick Collection of potential photographs from various assignments.

- Navigating my folders is a breeze using the grid view of the Library.
- Select the images I'm considering.
- To save time while adding photos to the Quick Collection, I like to utilize keyboard shortcuts. Click B or right-click and choose Save Quick Collection to accomplish this.
- After that, save the Quick Collection as a Collection.
- The next step is to go through the Collection and choose the pictures I want to use for the article.

To save a Quick Collection to a Collection:

- With the right mouse button, click on Quick Collection.

- Select **Save Quick Collection** from the menu that appears.

- Give your collection a name.

- Select **Clear Quick Collection After Saving** from the drop-down menu.

- If you want it to appear in your Collections panel, you can click **Save**.

3. **Target Collections**

To transform any ordinary collection into a Target Collection, Quick Collections are not required. To make a collection a target, you can do it by right-clicking on its name and selecting **Set as Target Collection** from the resulting menu.

After creating a Target Collection in Lightroom Classic, adding photographs to it is as easy as pressing a key or using a shortcut in the menu. Instead of adding the photo to the Quick Collection, it will be added straight to the Target Collection you've specified when you press the B key (or right-click and choose

Add to Target Collection). Without having to go through a bunch of choices, this function is great for rapidly grouping photos into a specific collection.

The second time you press the B key or right-click the photo, choose **Remove from Target Collection** from the menu, you can remove it from the Target Collection. The picture will still be in its original or other collections after this process deletes it from the Target Collection.

For all sorts of picture management and organization needs, Target Collections are a lifesaver. A Target Collection can be used for things like:

- Gather your client's favorite shots from the most recent session and make a list of them.

- To make keeping track of your choices easier, compile all the photos you want to use in a photo book.

- Make virtual copies of photos in the exact dimensions needed for Instagram stories and other social media sites, saving you time and effort while getting ready to post.

If you're using Lightroom Classic and have completed adding photographs to a Target Collection, you may simply delete the target feature. This will prevent you from adding new images to the collection whenever you hit the B key, but you will still be able to access and view the existing collection.

In the Collections panel, right-click the collection's name to delete the Target Collection feature. To turn off the collection's target functionality, go to the context menu that shows up and uncheck the box that says **Set as Target Collection.**

After you do this, the Quick Collection will revert to its original state before you set up the Target Collection for any additional photographs you choose and press B for. With this feature, you can streamline your process and avoid inadvertently adding outdated photographs to an existing collection.

4. **Smart Collections**

Lightroom automatically populates these collections based on their settings. There are six pre-configured smart collections in Lightroom:

- Colored Red (or whatever colors you've used)
- Five Stars

- Past Month
- Recently Modified
- Video Files
- Without Keywords

Using smart collections in Lightroom

You can use the metadata of your pictures to filter the Smart Collection, in addition to the default ones, to build your own. For example, you can compile all of your photos into a Smart Collection:

- With a particular lens
- On a particular day
- Or of a particular person

Many of the items on this list can be used to add images to a smart collection, whether they are already there in the metadata or are ones that you manually add, such as keywords or person tags.

Creating a Smart Collection is as follows:

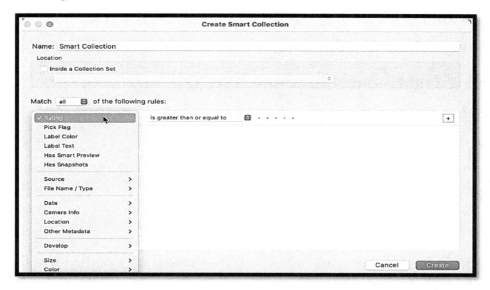

- There is a + sign next to Collections; click it.
- Select **Create Smart Collection** from the option that appears.
- Name the Smart Collection, configure its settings, and then hit **Create**.

What's the difference between a Collection and a Smart Collection in Lightroom?

Collections

- Images are added to Collections manually.
- You can rearrange pictures as much as you want in a regular Lightroom Collection.

Smart Collections

- Smart Collections are configured to compile images on their own. As an example, a Smart Collection can house all of your five-star images. You can see an image there if you give it five stars. Any change to the five-star rating will cause it to be removed from the Smart Collection.

- It is not possible to manually organize photos in a Smart Collection. You can still arrange them using the default settings for things like label color, star rating, and capture time.

Where are Lightroom collections stored?

The Collections panel, located on the left side of the screen, provides access to collections inside the Library and Develop modules.

Lightroom Collections do not hold image data. Quite similar to a method for retrieving a set of photos from several different collections or folders.

How do I organize my Lightroom collections?

Lightroom Collections can be individual Collections or can be organized into Collection Sets.

As an example, my portrait photography business and The Lens Lounge both have their own Collection Sets, which are further separated into Collection Sets for certain genres like boudoir, personal branding, and model portfolios.

How to create a Collection Set:
- Click the + symbol next to Collections.
- Select **Create Collection Set** from the drop-down menu.
- Give the Collection Set a name.

- If it's going into a Collection Set, you can specify which one it will go into by checking the box. If not, then deselect the box.

- Select **Create**

81

CHAPTER 6

WORKING WITH KEYWORDS AND METADATA

Applying Keywords

Keywords are a kind of user-added metadata that describe the contents of a picture. They are a great resource for learning where to look for certain images in the database. After applying XMP metadata to images, Adobe products like Adobe Bridge, PhotoShop, and Photoshop Elements can read the keywords.

Several methods exist in Lightroom Classic to add keywords to images. It's possible to type or choose keywords in the Keywording panel, or you can drag pictures to certain keywords in the Keyword List panel.

In the Grid view, a thumbnail badge will appear next to photos that include keywords. In the Keyword List panel, you can view all of the catalog's keywords. You have the freedom to add, edit, rename, or delete keywords whenever you choose. The ability to select synonyms and export options is available while creating or editing keywords. There is a close relationship between keywords and synonyms. Photos with related keywords will display those words in the Keywording window when you go to **Keyword > Will Export**.

Inside a keyword can be another keyword. Take animals as an example; it might contain both cats and dogs. Conversely, dogs might encompass a wide range of breeds, including Australian Shepherds, Border Collies, and more.

Create keywords

1. Select an image or images in the Filmstrip, then choose an option from the following in the Grid view, the Loupe, the Compare, or the Survey views:

    o   In the **Keywording** panel, locate the **Click Here To Add Keywords** box and input your keywords there. The next step is to hit the Enter

(Windows) or Return (Mac OS X) key. Do not proceed with the remaining steps of this procedure.

     ○   Press the plus symbol (+) in the **Keyword List** panel.

2.   The **Create Keyword Tag** box is where you can give the keyword a name.

3.   Type synonyms for the keyword. Separate each word with a comma.

4.   Please select one of the shown options.

Edit keywords

1.   Select a keyword from the Keyword List panel in the Library module by right-clicking (Windows) or control-clicking (Mac OS X). Pressing this will open a menu from which you can select **Edit Keyword Tag**.

2.   You can alter the name of the keyword, add synonyms, or set any of the given keyword possibilities inside the **Edit Keyword Tag** box.

Export Synonyms

When exporting photographs, it also includes synonyms that are related to the term.

Rename keywords

1.   Select a keyword from the **Keyword List** panel in the Library module by right-clicking (Windows) or control-clicking (Mac OS X). Pressing this button will open a menu from which you can select **Edit Keyword Tag**.

2.   Change the keyword's name in the **Edit Keyword Tag** box before clicking **Save**.

Adding keywords to photos

The Library module has a **Keywording** panel where you can add keywords to images. Either enter a new keyword or select one from a list. Additionally, you can add keywords to images by dragging and dropping them into the **Keyword List** window. Unless you select the **Automatically Write Changes Into XMP** option in the **Catalog Settings** dialog box, Lightroom Classic will store your keyword photo edits locally rather than saving them to the files. Go to **Metadata** and choose **Save Metadata To File** to manually save the keywords.

1. Select all the images you wish to add keywords to in the Grid view simultaneously. Additionally, in Loupe, Compare, or Survey view, you have the option to select a single image from the Filmstrip.

   Note: Take note that in Loupe, Compare, and Survey views, you can choose several images from the Filmstrip. Only the active photo will have the keywords added to it.

2. Perform one of the following:

   o Press the **Click Here To Add Keywords** button in the Keywords area of the **Keywording** panel and enter your keywords. Put commas to separate keywords. Using |, <, or > will display a hierarchy of keywords. Here are several examples: animal | dog, animal > dog, or dog < animal.

   o Choose a keyword from the **Keyword Suggestions** section of the **Keywording** panel. When generating keyword suggestions, several factors are considered, including the number of times the selected image and similar images from the same period have been used.

   o In the **Keyword Set** area of the **Keywording** panel, click on a keyword from a keyword set.

   o Locate the target box to the left of a keyword in the Keyword List panel. Click on it. A checkmark indicates that the selected image contains the specified keyword.

   o In the Keyword List panel, drag photographs to keywords (only works in Grid view). The Keyword List panel also allows you to drag and drop keywords onto your selected images.

   Note: Please be aware that Lightroom Classic allows you to add keywords to imported images.

When you add keywords to photographs, the Keyword List panel displays how many photos have that tag.

Copy and paste keywords

1. In the Grid view, locate the image containing the keywords you wish to copy.

2. For Windows users, right-click the selected keywords in the applied tags section of the Keywording panel. For Mac OS X users, control-click. Then, choose **Copy**.

3. Select the images you wish to add keywords in the Grid view.

4. Choose **Paste** from the menu that appears when you right-click (Windows) or control-click (Mac OS X) on the applied tags section of the Keywording panel.

Remove or delete keywords from photos or the catalog

1. Select an image or images from the Grid view. If you're in the Survey, Compare, or Loupe view, pick a picture from the Filmstrip and then do:

   o To delete keywords from photographs, go to the **Keywording** panel and choose **Keyword Tags > Enter Keywords**. The next step is to choose a keyword or keywords and delete them from the panel's text area. When in Loupe, Compare, or Survey view, you can select several images from the Filmstrip. Only the current photo will have the keywords removed.

   o Click the keyword in the **Keyword List** panel with the right mouse button (Windows) or control-click (Mac OS X) and then choose **Delete** from the menu that appears. By doing so, the keyword will be permanently removed from both the images and the catalog. You can also pick keywords and click the minus sign (-) at the top of the **Keyword List** panel.

Note: If you accidentally delete keywords, immediately hit Ctrl+Z (Windows) or Command+Z (Mac OS X) to undo the action.

o   Unused keywords may be removed from the catalog by going to **Metadata > Purge Unused Keywords.**

Note: You will not be able to retrieve deleted keywords once you have executed the Purge Unused Keywords command.

After you remove keywords from images, the number of photos that still use the tag is shown in the Keyword List panel.

Add or remove keywords using the Painter tool

Using the Painter tool, you can quickly add keywords to your photographs after you've configured keyword shortcuts in Lightroom Classic. The best way to utilize it is as follows:

1. **Enable the Painter Tool:**

    o   If the Painter tool isn't showing up in the Library module's toolbar, you can make it available by navigating to **Metadata** and then choosing **Enable Painting**.

    o   Alternatively, you can access the Painter tool from the toolbar directly in Grid view. To make it visible, you might have to add it to your toolbar.

    Your pointer will transform into a paintbrush symbol as soon as you launch the Painter tool. If you're still having trouble seeing the Painter symbol in the toolbar, make sure it is enabled from the menu.

2. **Select Keywords:**

    Select **Keywords** from the Painter tool's menu if you wish to apply that. You may now annotate your chosen images with specific keywords.

3.   **Enter Keywords:**

In the toolbar box, type in the keyword (or keywords) you want to use. The images you choose using the Painter tool will have these keywords applied to them.

4.   **Apply Keywords:**

    o   **Single Photo:** To apply the keyword to a single image, use the Painter tool and click on a single photo.

    o   **Multiple Photos:** Click and drag across multiple photos in the Grid view to apply the keyword to all chosen images.

    o   **Remove Keywords:** Holding down the Alt key on Windows or the Option key on Mac OS can cause the Painter tool to transition to an eraser mode, allowing you to remove keywords. Click on the photo or drag across several photos to remove the keyword.

Tip: One helpful hint is to use the white arrow next to the keyword in the Keyword List panel to swiftly filter photographs in Grid view based on that phrase. You can easily evaluate or remove photographs by displaying only those that include that keyword.

5.   **Turn Off Painter Tool:**

    o   Once you're done, click the **circular well** in the Painter tool menu to disable it. The Painter icon will reappear in the toolbar, indicating that the tool is turned off.

You can quickly manage keywords across all of your photographs with the Painter tool, which will help you keep your catalog structured and searchable.

Working with keyword sets and nesting keywords

It is in the Keyword Set area of the Keywording panel that you manage keyword sets. A keyword set is a group of keywords that have been purposefully constructed. Sort the keywords you'll need for the project into three categories: special occasion, project, and family and friends. Lightroom Classic comes with three main groups of keyword presets.

Feel free to put these sets to whatever purpose you see fit. They can serve as a foundation for your setups. Having a keyword set on hand is a lifesaver when you're responsible for managing many library collections. A keyword tag can belong to multiple keyword sets. Select the **Presets** tab in **Lightroom's Preferences** window. The Lightroom presets may be accessed through the Keyword Set menu. Hit the **Restore Keyword Set Presets** button on the **Lightroom Defaults** menu. This section will make use of examples, so bear that in mind.

The steps:

1. The Keyword Set space in the Keywording panel can be enlarged if necessary. Then, under the Keyword Set menu, choose Wedding Photography. This list of keywords will make organizing the images from a large event a breeze. To find out what other categories Lightroom has to offer, have a look at their other keyword sets. By customizing these templates, you can create your groups of keywords and save them as a new preset. An excellent method to maintain order is to build up sets of keywords. To keep them organized, you can arrange the tags in a tree-like structure according to their connections.

2. In the Keyword List panel, look for the **Syracuse keyword**. Place it on top of the New York keyword by dragging it. The New York keyword expands to reveal the Syracuse tag nestled inside it in an instant.

3.   Transfer your files to the Collections keyword from the keywords list. You can see the nested tags when you expand the Collections tag.

4.   I propose enhancing the Tour keyword with the Chicago term to display certain images. If you want to add more keywords to the Tour category, go to the Keyword List panel and click the addition symbol (+) in the top left.

5.   Click Create after you've entered **Chicago** into the **Keyword Name** field of the Keyword Tag dialog box and verify that the first three options under Keyword Tag Options are selected (as seen in the image below).

o   Recall to add the keyword tag when you export your images.

o   The parent tag, which contains keywords, is included in the photo export.

o   While you're exporting your photographs, the export synonyms feature will add any terms that are related to the keyword tag.

6.   Select a folder from the Folders panel. After that, choose all of the images in that folder except the final two. You can use the Chicago keyword tag from the Keyword List to enhance any of the images you've selected in the Grid view.

If you're looking for a way to export or import keywords, I recommend going to the Metadata menu. You can use them to transfer keyword lists across devices or share them with other Lightroom users. As you peruse the Keyword List, be sure to put checkmarks next to the newly added Chicago and Tour keyword categories. Next to each entry, you can also check the number of photographs on the right. All the selected images have these two keyword tags applied to them.

Searching by keyword

Ratings, flags, and labels are examples of metadata that can be used to correctly organize your photographs. Next, you can easily locate the precise photo you're looking for by configuring advanced filters. Using keyword searches or filters, you can locate images in your collection. If you want to use both sets of side panels at once, you can do that by right-clicking on the group's header and unchecking **Solo mode** from the option that displays.

Here are the steps:

1. Select **Library > Show Photos In Subfolders** if you haven't done so before. To make room for the Catalog and Folder panels, you can collapse any of the other panels in the left panel's group. Either use **Command+D/Ctrl+D** or click on the folder in the Folders menu and then choose **Edit > Select None**.

2. Resize the thumbnails by using the Thumbnails slider on the toolbar. More photographs will be seen in the Grid view after this. You can display the Filter bar above the Grid view by selecting **View > Show Filter Bar** or by using the Backslash key (\).

3. Collapse the other panels in the right panel group as needed to display the enlarged Keyword List panel's contents.

4. Click the white arrow that appears next to the image count when you hover over the other keyword in the Keyword List screen.

   Your whole catalog was searched for photographs with the keyword tag you opened, as seen by the fact that All Photographs are picked in the left panel group. In the Filter bar located at the top of the workspace, you can see that the Metadata filter has been active. From now on, the Grid view will only display photos in your collection that include the opened keyword tag.

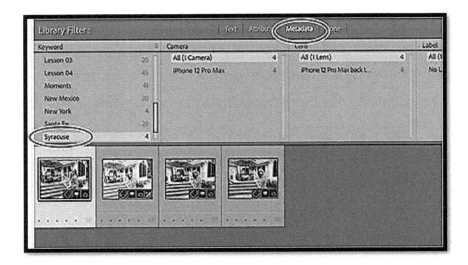

Only four of the tagged images will appear in the Grid view. You will search differently now.

5.   To begin, locate the **All** category under the **Keywords** column. Then, go to the **Filter bar** on top and choose **Text**. Choose **Any Searchable Field** from the first menu and **Contains All** from the second menu. Carefully consider all of the menu items. Next, use the box on the right to input **Tour** and then hit **Enter** or **Return**.

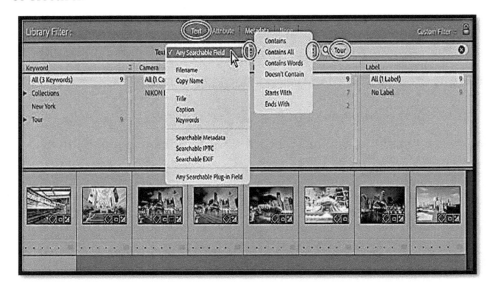

Tip: As you go to different image sources in the Catalog, Folders, or Collections panel, remember to press the lock button on the right side of the Filter bar. Your present filter settings will be preserved. There are currently nine images available in the Grid view. More complex filters based on a combination of criteria make the most of the Library's filters. Your actions need to have demonstrated the range of possibilities.

6. Select **None** from the Filter bar's upper-right corner to disable all filters. From the Folders panel, choose the folder. Go to **Edit > Select None**, or use **Command+D** or **Ctrl+D**.

Using flags and ratings

You can easily locate and arrange your images using the Attribute filters located in the Filter bar. Some of the criteria used to create these filters include ratings and flags. The Attribute button will enlarge the Library Filter bar. This will show controls to sort images by flag status, edit status, star rating, color label, copy status, or any combination of these.

Flagging images

To start assembling a set of images, you can add flags to distinguish between excellent and bad images, as well as between marked and untagged images. A picture can be marked as a pick, rejected, or left unflagged.

Follow these steps:

1. At the very top of the Filter bar, click on **Attribute**. When the Filter bar becomes larger, the controls for the Attribute filter become visible. In both the Grid and Loupe views, you can use the Toolbar to add ratings, flags, and color

labels. In the Compare and Survey views, you can adjust any of these settings using the buttons located beneath the images. You have the option to flag, rate, or color label a chosen picture in the Photo menu.

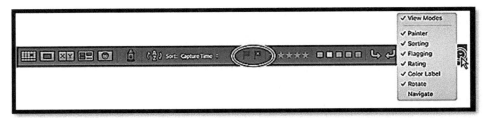

2. To bring up the Toolbar beneath the Grid view, just hit the **T** key. To access the Flagging menu, press the **triangle** located on the Toolbar's right side; this will show the Flag as Pick and Set as Rejected buttons in the Toolbar.

3. Use the Folders panel to locate and choose a folder.

4. Select an image from this collection while in Grid view. A gray flag symbol will show up in the upper left corner of the picture cell if you select the Flags option under Cell Icons in the **Library View Options** dialog box. At this time, the image is untagged. If the flag symbol isn't showing up, try hovering your cursor over the picture cell or disabling the setting in the Library View Options box that makes clickable objects only appear when the mouse is hovered over them. To access the **View Options** box, either press **Command+J** or **Ctrl+J,** or navigate to **View > View Options**.

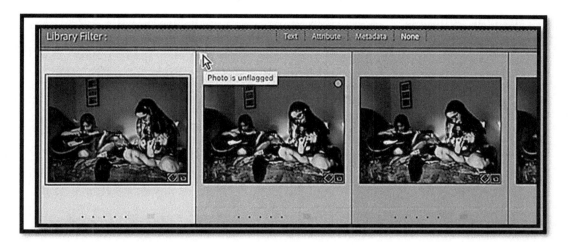

5. There is now a white flag symbol in the upper left corner of the image cell that you can use to designate the flag as Flagged. You can also use the Flag as Pick button on the Toolbar or click on the flag badge inside the image cell.

6. To access the Attribute Filter, use the white flag icon. Only the flagged image is displayed in the Grid view. From the folder you accessed, the screen now only displays the marked photographs.

   TIP: Navigate to **Library** > **Refine Photos** to swiftly arrange your photographs according to whether they have been marked or not. Navigate to **Library** > **Refine Photos** and then click **Refine** in the **Refine Photos** box. Doing so will return the selected photographs to their unflagged state and classify all non-flagged ones as rejections.

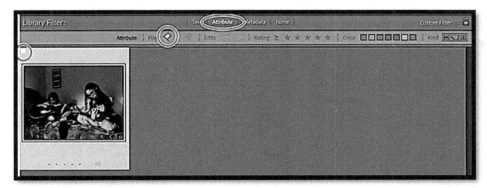

In Lightroom Classic 2025, you can make notes on a picture in several different ways. Press the P key on your keyboard or go to **Photo > Set Flag > Flagged** to make a picture a pick. To go from **Unflagged** to **Pick**, locate the flag symbol in the upper left corner of the photo cell and click on it. Find Photo > Set Flag > refused and press the X key. You can also option-click or alt-press the flag icon in the upper left corner of the image cell to mark it as refused.

To remove a flag from an image, either press the U key or navigate to Photo > Set Flag > Unflagged. To flag, unflag, or reject a picture, just right-click on the flag symbol in the upper left corner of the cell. A new flag state has been applied to the picture.

7. Verify that the white flag is still selected in the Attribute Filter bar. After that, go to the center and click on the **gray flag** button. All the images in the Sabine-guitar folder are now viewable in the Grid view, including those that have been tagged as picks and those that have not.

8. Attribute filters can be disabled by selecting None from the Filter bar.

Assigning ratings

As you go through each photo, rating it from one to five stars will help you store them all in one place.

Follow these steps:

1. Click on a folder in the Folders panel. Verify that the Sort option on the Toolbar is set to Capture Time in the Grid view. Then, to choose it, click on the second image.

2. Pressing the 3 key on your keyboard will cause the words **Set Rating To 3** to appear on the screen for a short while. Three stars now appear in the picture cell's bottom left corner. Verify that **Rating And Label** is selected in the

Bottom Label or Top Label option in the Compact Cell Extras display settings under View > View Options to ensure that the stars are seen.

3. To edit the rating, locate the triangle in the Toolbar's right-hand corner and, from the drop-down menu that displays, choose **Rating**. The most recent rating for the currently chosen image is displayed by the stars in the Toolbar. The Toolbar will display the rating of the initially selected image if multiple images with different ratings are selected. Either select Photo > Set Rating from the contextual menu that displays or right-click on a photo's thumbnail to access the rating options in the Metadata panel.

4. Quickly assign a new rating to a selected image by pressing a key between 1 and 5, or erase the rating by pressing 0. For this image, press the **0** key.

Applying Metadata

Metadata refers to the information that is associated with picture files. Your photo collection will be easier to manage and arrange with its guidance. Metadata, such as the time and date of the capture, the duration of the exposure, the focal length, and the camera settings, are automatically generated by your camera. To further improve catalog organization and search capabilities, you have the option to add your metadata.

It demonstrated your expertise that you tagged your photographs with keywords, ratings, and color labels. Information standards like those established by the

International Press Telecommunications Council (IPTC) are adhered to by Lightroom as well. These standards address issues, such as credits, category, description, and origin. In the right-hand panel group, you'll find the Metadata panel, which allows you to see or edit picture metadata.

Follow these steps:

1. Select the folder containing your pictures in the Folders panel. Just choose any image you like in the Grid view.

    At the very bottom of the Metadata panel, on the Metadata Set menu, you'll see a Customize button. It's adjacent to the Default setting. You can choose which fields to display in that configuration by clicking on it.

2. Hiding the Filmstrip or collapsing the other panels in the right panel group will allow you to see the Metadata panel better. After you see the Metadata panel header, look for the Metadata Set menu and select **Default**.

    A great deal of picture information is displayed by the default metadata configuration. You can also add data from a plethora of other areas by clicking the Customize button. Much of the information, which is useful for organizing your photographs, was created by the camera itself. Sorting images by date of capture, finding images shot with a specific lens, or identifying differences between images captured by various cameras are just a few examples. By default, just a subset of an image's metadata is displayed.

3. Select **EXIF** and **IPTC** from the Metadata Set menu. Go to the next page of the Metadata panel to learn about the different kinds of data that can be added to a picture.

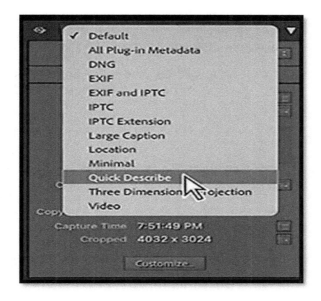

4. Select **Quick Describe** from the Metadata Set menu to complete the process. Details such as the filename, folder, rating, and EXIF and IPTC metadata from the Quick Describe set are shown in the Metadata panel. A virtual copy's name is also displayed. Change the star rating, add a copyright notice, share the photo's location and photographer, and add a caption and title all from this panel.

5. On the Metadata panel, you can see the Rating button; click on it to give the photo three stars. Then, in the Title text box, put Sabine and Ethan in the Game and hit **Return** or **Enter**.

6. To include one of the two similarly styled images in your collection, just click on it. Next, go to the top of the Metadata panel and click on **Selected Photos**. The folder names, sizes, and camera models of the two files are identical. But now, <mixed> will appear for items that neither image has. Although the values of the selected photos may differ, any changes made to the Metadata panel will affect both of them.

To get a more comprehensive caption for your files, go for the Large Caption Metadata Set. Photojournalists and sports photographers should pay close attention to this. It will be easier to compose the title as you will have more area for it.

Storing metadata

The XML-based Extensible Metadata Platform (XMP) standard is used for data storage. Since camera raw files use their format, XMP is not pre-installed for dealing with these files.

Metadata may be easily transferred across different Adobe applications and publication processes thanks to this functionality. By importing information from one file and utilizing it as a model in other files, you may speed up your work. To facilitate viewing and management, XMP is employed to characterize and synchronize information kept in various formats, such as EXIF, IPTC (IIM), and TIFF.

CHAPTER 7

PHOTO EDITING ESSENTIALS

White Balance

The term used to describe the level of light intensity in an image is **white balance**. Various sources of light, such as natural light, artificial light, and even clouded sky, can alter the appearance of colors in a photograph. Changing the white balance is as simple as adjusting the color's temperature and tint to your liking. When you're in the Basic panel, choose the file you want to edit, then choose **As Shot** underneath WB at the top. Adjust the white balance sliders to see what works best for you.

When shooting in raw format, you'll have access to more menu options than when shooting in JPEG. You will find these choices in your camera. Determine which one best mimics the lighting conditions in the area where you shot the photo. Additionally, you may make adjustments using the Temp and Tint sliders.

TIP: Although the White Balance menu gives you access to white balance settings in raw pictures, using the White Balance Selector is often quicker. Because your camera has already established the white balance for JPEGs, there are fewer options for them in this menu.

Like an eyedropper, the White Balance Selector appears on the screen. If you're not satisfied with the outcome, you may access the White Balance Selector in the Basic panel by clicking or pressing the W button on your computer. Hover your mouse over the image and click on a patch of neutral hue, such as a light or medium gray area. A neutral shade may be discovered with the use of the popping-up loupe.

About white balance

Maintaining a uniform distribution of colors in a photograph is essential for accurately displaying the color information included in the file. Resetting the white balance of the camera is another name for this process.

To do this, the white point of the picture is adjusted. Below, on the right side of the picture, you can see a curving line representing temperature (blue to red) and tint (green to magenta), which both revolve around the white point, which is the neutral point.

The white point shows the lighting conditions when the shot was taken. Varying types of artificial lighting have varying white points, thus the light they produce leans heavily toward one hue or the other. The weather can also affect the white balance.

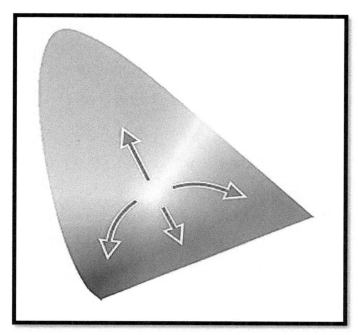

The hue temperature of the image is determined by a shift along this axis, whereas shifts in the magenta or green direction are referred to as tints. A greater red component of the lighting will make the colors in the shot appear warmer, while a higher blue component will make the colors look cooler.

To capture an object's red, green, and blue light reflection, a digital camera uses sensors. All the hues in the light source are uniformly reflected when pure white light is shone on gray, black, or white objects.

More green light will be reflected while using fluorescent lighting, as the light source is mostly green, rather than pure white. Even objects that shouldn't have a hue cast can, if you alter the white balance or white point to match the light source's composition without knowing what it is.

By analyzing the color data collected by the sensors, your camera attempts to determine the kind of light source when you switch to auto white balance mode. Modern cameras do a better job of automatically detecting the lighting conditions and adjusting the white balance accordingly, but the technology is far from ideal. Take a reading of the white point of the light source before snapping a photo if your camera has that capability. Typically, a white or neutral-colored object in the same environment as the person is photographed to get this effect.

In addition to the color information received by the camera's sensors, raw photos also contain As Shot white balance data, which documents the automated white point selection made by the camera throughout the shooting process. With this data, Lightroom can learn how to interpret the recorded color data for a given light source more accurately. The captured white point information will be used to adjust the picture's color balance relative to a calibration point.

To set Lightroom to adjust all of the colors to a neutral point, you may tell it which color is neutral (pure gray) using the **White Balance Selector**. In the WB panel, the tool resembles an eyedropper, and all it takes to select it is a click.

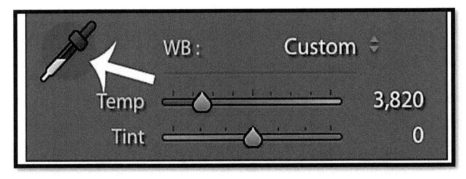

An enlarged view of the pixels beneath the eyedropper and the RGB values for the central target pixel may be obtained by dragging the White Balance Selector tool over the image.

To avoid a drastic shift in hue, click on a pixel with closely spaced red, green, and blue numbers. Avoid using white or other extremely bright colors, such as spectral highlights, for the neutral purpose. In a very bright pixel, one or more of the color components may have already been cut.

Described by the term blackbody radiation theory is the color temperature. When heated, a blackbody's glow will go from red to orange to yellow to white and eventually blue-white. In kelvins, the temperature at which a black body emits a certain color is called the color temperature. One degree Celsius is equivalent to one kelvin, and it's worth mentioning that zero K is equal to -273.15°C or -459.67°F.

Our typical mental image of a warm hue is one with a stronger red component. Color temperatures (in kelvin) are inversely proportional to the proportion of blue in cool hues. A warmly illuminated room with candles has a color temperature of around 1500 K. In direct sunlight, the color temperature would be around 5500 K, however, in overcast skies, it would range from 6000 to 7000 K.

You may adjust the white point's color temperature (in kelvin) using the Temperature slider. To the left of the slider is a low point, and to the right is a high point. A leftward shift in the Temp tool lowers the white point's color temperature. The result is a shift toward blue in the image's color temperature, which is greater than the new white point. You can see the effect on the image's coloration when you drag the Temp slider control. The image will appear bluer if you shift the scale to the left. Shifting it to the right will make the reds and yellows pop out more in the image.

The Tint slider works in the same way. By dragging the Tint slider to the right, away from the green displayed inside the slider control, you may remove a green tint from a photo. As a result of the white point being made greener, the colors in the picture appear to have less green tones than before.

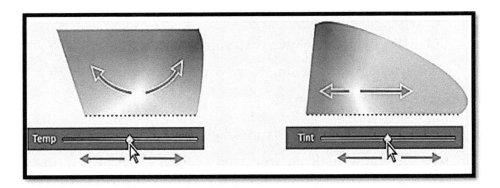

You can adjust the white point's location in the color space by using the Temp and Tint sliders.

To begin editing images with Adobe Lightroom Classic, you must first adjust the color temperature and white balance. Changing these settings is as easy as following these steps:

1. **Enter the Develop Module:**

   To access the Develop module in Lightroom Classic, open the program and click on the Develop tab located at the top of the screen.

2. **Find the Controls for White Balance:**

   On the Basic panel's right side is the White Balance section.

3. **Pick a White Balance Preset:**

   There are several white balance presets available in Lightroom Classic, including Auto, Daylight, Cloudy, Shade, Tungsten, and Fluorescent. Next to White Balance is a drop-down menu; from there, select the option that corresponds best with the ambient light in the shot.

4. **Use the Temperature Slider:**

   If you're not satisfied with the presets, you can manually adjust the color temperature using the Temperature slider.

   To make the image more inviting, drag the slider towards the right (yellow). Shift it to the left (in the direction of blue) to make it cooler.

5. **Fine-Tune with the Tint Slider:**

    On the right side of the Temperature slider is the Tint slider, which allows you to alter the magenta-green balance of your image. Just a little adjustment to the right will give you a magenta hue. Just slide it to the left to make it green.

6. **Use the Eyedropper Tool (Optional):**

    Select the WB Selector tool—it resembles an eyedropper—to adjust the white balance.

    Find a white or gray area in your image and click on it. Lightroom will automatically adjust the white balance if you select that option.

7. **Apply Graduated and Radial Filters:**

    Using Graduated Filters or Radial Filters could help you make adjustments in a smaller area. You can electively adjust the white balance of an area in your image with these tools.

8. **Sync White Balance Settings (Optional):**

    For all your photos captured in the same lighting circumstances, you can configure the white balance to be the same. Then, right-click on a few images on the film strip and select Sync Settings.

9. **Check Before and After Views:**

    Click the \ key to toggle between the before and after displays, allowing you to observe the impact of your white balance adjustments.

10. **Save Presets (Optional):**

    If you frequently encounter similar lighting circumstances, you have the option to save your white balance adjustments as a preference for future reference. Navigate to the + symbol that appears next to the Presets box, and then select Create Preset.

11. **Fine-Tune in HSL/Color Panel (Optional):**

The HSL/Color panel allows for finer-grained customization of each color channel. In the HSL/Color panel, you can adjust the Hue, Saturation, and Luminance variables for each color.

12. **Reset White Balance (If Needed):**

To restore the original white balance, either click the WB name in the Basic panel or double-click the Temperature and Tint sliders.

Follow these instructions to adjust Lightroom Classic's color temperature and white balance. Doing so will guarantee that the colors and lighting in your images turn out just how you envisioned them.

How to use the histogram

Disputes over the histograms of your Lightroom photographs may quickly escalate into furious arguments. People often say that the histogram in images should be retained **as a curve** or, worse, that the right-hand histogram is the **perfect** one. While familiarity with histograms is necessary, it is of utmost importance to remember that they should only be used in a descriptive rather than an analytical capacity.

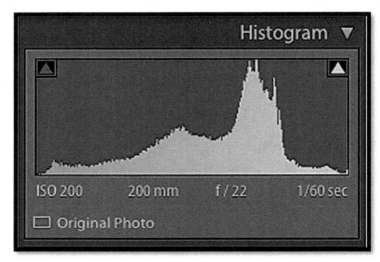

This is going to seem simplistic, but picture a histogram as a chart. On the left side of the histogram, you can see several dots that don't have any brightness. All of the dots on the right are fully illuminated. In the white space, you can observe color values ranging from 0 to 255. Here we see the range of values from darkest to lightest.

Among Adobe Lightroom Classic's many helpful features, the histogram stands out. It lays out all the different tones in your image for you. The distribution of highlights, midtones, and blacks is depicted in the picture.

Lightroom Classic's histogram provides a graphical representation of the distribution of tones in your image. It reveals the distribution of tones, with mid tones in the center, shadows to the left, and highlights to the right. You can improve your editing options by learning to utilize and comprehend the histogram. You can use the histogram in Lightroom Classic for the following:

1. **Open the Histogram:**

    On the right side of the Basic panel at the top of the Develop module is where you can see the histogram.

2. **An Overview of the Histogram**:

    The histogram is a graph with shades of black on the left and white on the right. The graph's peaks and valleys show how the tones in your picture are spread out.

3. **RGB Channels:**

    A red, green, and blue version of the graph is available. To navigate between stations, just click on the little triangles that appear above the histogram. It is configured to display the RGB mixed view.

4. **Highlight and Shadow Clipping Indicators:**

Drag the cursor across the graph to activate the highlight and shadow clipping indications. Red will indicate too bright regions on the right and blue will indicate underexposed areas on the left.

5. **Adjust Exposure Using the Histogram:**

In the Basic panel, you can adjust the overall exposure by dragging the black and white sliders. As you adjust these sliders, the histogram will update to reflect the changes, and the clipping indications will highlight potential areas of data loss.

6. **Use Tone Curve for Precision:**

To make more intricate adjustments to the tone, you can use the Tone Curve panel. By utilizing the histogram present in the Tone Curve panel, you can selectively alter particular tonal bands.

7. **Histogram Peaks and Valleys:**

Where there are many tones, the histogram will show it as a peak; where there are fewer tones, it will show it as a valley. You can learn about the distribution of tones in your shot by observing these patterns.

8. **Evaluate Color Balance:**

In addition to displaying brightness, the histogram can also aid in determining color balance. If the RGB channels' peaks aren't equally distributed, a color shift might occur.

9. **Checking for Clipping:**

Verify that neither the shadows nor the highlights are clipped. Adjust the exposure and tone sliders such that the histogram stays away from the extremes. If this occurs, it indicates that either the shadows or the highlights are becoming less detailed.

10. **Histogram as a Guideline:**

Though helpful, the histogram is not an absolute rule. To achieve a certain artistic look, it is often necessary to intentionally shift tones beyond the typical histogram range.

11. **Histogram for Batch Editing:**

The histogram is a great tool to have on hand when dealing with many images at once; it allows you to easily verify that each one has the same exposure settings.

12. **Before and After Views:**

To go from the **before** to the **after** view, use the \ key. You can observe the effects of your edits to the histogram in this way.

If you want to know how the tones in your photo are spread and make wise editing choices, learn how to utilize the histogram in Lightroom Classic. To get balanced and pleasing results when editing, refer to the histogram frequently.

Adjusting exposure, contrast, and saturation

In f-stops, the amount of light that a lens lets in is represented, while exposure is determined by the amount of light that a camera's sensor picks up. To expose one stop more than the camera's settings, use the scale +1.00, which functions similarly to a camera's stops. Portrait skin tones are considered mid-tones, and their brightness may be adjusted using Lightroom's Exposure slider. To adjust the brightness, simply move the scale to the right to make it brighter, and to the left to make it darker. The right side is white, while the left side is black.

1. After you've chosen your image, move the Exposure slider to the right until it reads +0.90. This makes the picture brighter right away.

2. Point the middle of the right-hand panel's histogram with your mouse. In addition to the phrase Exposure appearing beneath the bottom left corner of

the histogram, a light gray region will be marked when the Exposure slider is adjusted.

As you can see in the image below, the data distribution was on the left side of the histogram before the adjustment. As can be observed in the image on the right, everything shifted to the right when the exposure was adjusted.

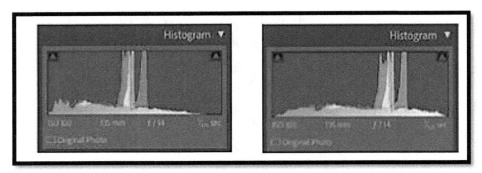

Lightroom will automatically adjust the slider wherever it is in the adjustment panels when you Shift-double-click on it. It will be much easier to establish the contrast if you opt to manually adjust the brightness and contrast rather than utilizing the Auto option. If you disregard contrast, you will easily muck up your shadows and highlights.

The contrast adjusts the level of brightness between the darkest and brightest areas of your image. The data on the histogram can be **stretched out** by dragging this tool to the right. As a result, the whites get brighter and the blacks become darker. What this means is that it's equivalent to halving the histogram at the center.

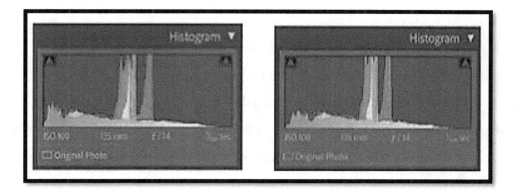

3. The contrast is reduced when the slider is moved to the left. Because of this, the histogram's data becomes compressed, resulting in a flattened or muddy appearance of the photo's tones caused by the narrowing of the distance between the blackest and whitest regions.

4. See what happens when you experiment with different brightness levels for the image. The image below shows the sliders for Exposure and Contrast set to +0.90 and +37, respectively. Because of this, the image is more noticeable.

5. To view the image both before and after the adjustment, use the Y key. After this, you will have a clear picture of the file's progress. This is one of the nicest parts of working with raw files while creating images.

Adjusting shadows and highlights

You can restore lost details using the sliders for Highlights and Shadows. Clipping occurs when one area of an image is either very bright or dark. Too much darkness (sometimes termed blocked) prevents details from being shown in the shadows. It's too black, too muddy, and not good. What this signifies is that there is a lack of clarity in certain areas where the highlights are too bright, a phenomenon known as blown out.

TIP: To toggle clipping warnings on and off, hit the **J** key on your keyboard.

In most cases, aim to capture as much detail in the shadows and highlights as you can without affecting the overall composition. The picture below was created by intentionally underexposing the camera so that the highlights would remain intact. Nevertheless, there was still a lack of detail at the bottom of the image. We should consult Shadows for advice.

1. Open the image. When you hover your mouse over the warning about shadow clipping in the top left corner of the histogram, you'll see that the clipped

shadows in your image become blue. The red highlights indicate blown-out highlights when you hover your mouse over the histogram or activate the warning about highlights clipping in the top right corner. To view the warnings, you can experiment by adjusting the Exposure. Next, enter +1.40 for the Exposure.

2. You can adjust the amount of data you get from the sky and the area surrounding the pond by dragging the Shadows slider to the right. It is recommended to use a value of +100.

115

3. To change the highlight scale to -100, click on a different photo. As a bonus, it brings a new hue to the sky, which enhances the appearance of the clouds.

4. Finalize the shot by adjusting the Shadows to +100 and the Exposure to -0.70. Last but not least, increase the temperature to +6950.

Take note of what the Shadows and Highlights settings do not do before attempting to use them. Colors are unaffected by dragging the Shadows slider. No matter where you drag the Highlights tool, the shades will remain fixed. That is some very powerful stuff.

Creating a black-and-white matte look

A matte black-and-white effect with a vintage, faded appearance requires a few adjustments in Lightroom Classic. To get this result, follow these steps:

1. **Open the picture in the Develop module:** After importing your image into Lightroom Classic, open it in the Develop module to begin working on the image.

2. **Change to black and white:** Pick Black & White from the Treatment menu on the Basic panel's right side to convert your image to black and white.

3. **Adjust the Tone Curve:** Make a soft S shape in the Tone Curve panel. To create a subtle fade, slightly increase the blacks and decrease the brightness. A matte finish can be achieved more easily with this.

4. **Adjust Contrast and Highlights:** Play around with the Basic panel's Contrast tool to adjust the highlights and contrast. To achieve a more vintage vibe, try using a less contrasting background. To make some areas less brilliant, you can drag the Highlights slider to the bottom.

5. **Fine-Tune Shadows and Blacks:** To soften the image by raising the darker areas, drag the Shadows slider. To lessen the effect, you can also adjust the black slider slightly.

6. **Apply Split Toning (Optional):** You can optionally apply split toning to the shadows and highlights using the Split Toning panel. Applying a cool tone to the shadows and a warm one to the highlights will create an aged, matte effect in your photo.

7. **Adjust Clarity and Texture:** To soften the image's appearance by reducing the mid-tone contrast, drag the Clarity slider down. You can also adjust the texture in the same way. You can tweak the finer points by experimenting with the Texture slider.

8. **Add Grain:** Get a film-like grain effect by using the Amount slider under Grain in the Effects panel. You can alter the appearance of the grain using the Size and Roughness settings.

9. **Vignette:** Use a vignette to highlight the focal point of your image. Modifying the Effects panel's Amount and Midpoint sliders will create a subtle vignette.

10. **Fine-Tune White Balance (Optional):** If you want to alter the black-and-white conversion's tone, you can do so by adjusting the overall color temperature.

11. **Apply Post-Crop Vignetting (Optional):** If you want to take the vignetting effect to the next level, you can utilize the Effects panel's Post-Crop Vignetting settings. This is how you alter the vignette's shape and shading.

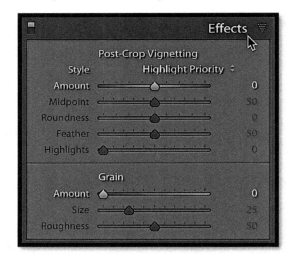

12. **Experiment and Save as Preset:** To acquire the effect you desire, play around with the parameters and save them as a preset. These settings can be saved as a preset, allowing you to apply them to other photographs in the future.

13. **Compare Before and After:** To compare the appearance of your modifications before and after, use the \ key to toggle between the **before** and **after** views.

Doing so, along with experimenting with Lightroom Classic's settings, will allow you to give your photographs a soft, vintage, black-and-white appearance. The overall appearance of the picture is affected by various adjustments made to its tone curves, contrast, vignetting, and other aspects.

Using dodge and burn for black-and-white photos

Import and Basic Adjustments

- Launch Adobe Lightroom Classic and bring in your monochrome image.
- Prioritize the changes required in the Develop module. To obtain a decent baseline, adjust the exposure, contrast, highlights, and blacks.
- Locate the **Develop module** by clicking on Develop in the upper right corner.
- To access the Adjustment Brush tool , locate it on the screen's right side and press the **K** key on your computer.

Dodge (Brighten) with Adjustment Brush

- Change how the Dodge brush works. Focus extra light (exposure) on areas that are already well-lit.
- Altering additional factors, such as Highlights and Whites, allows you to alter the appearance if desired.
- Gently scrub the areas you wish to improve. Typically, highlights are used for this purpose, since they accentuate objects in areas of higher brightness.
- Reduce the brush opacity to weaken the dodge effect if it's too intense.

Using an adjustment brush to burn (Darken)

- To set the brush, select **Burn**. Reduce Your Exposure to Dim Areas.
- You have the option to adjust the Blacks and Shadows to make the appearance more or less what you like.
- To add depth to your photo and highlight features in shadows, use a brush.

- To adjust the intensity of the burn effect, you can adjust the brush's brightness, similar to Dodge.

Graduated filters for dodge and burn

- Click on **M** to bring the Graduated Filter tool. From there, you can gradually increase the brightness of the photo with this tool. Simply slide the filter from the lighter to the darker region in that direction.
- To get an effect where the hue gradually darkens, similarly apply the Graduated Filter. Drag the dark region to bring it closer to the light region.

Fine-tune with radial filters

Dodge and Burn Dial Filter:

Pressing **Shift+M** and utilizing radial filters allows you to adjust the brightness or darkness of certain areas inside your image. Adjust the parameters as required.

Refine and Review:

- Get a closer look at your edits and refine them until they're flawless. Verify that the details are brought out by the burn and dodge techniques without losing information or making the image overly bright.
- You can toggle between the original and modified versions with the backslash key (/). You can observe the effects of your dodge and burn adjustments in this way.
- You have the option to adjust the overall sharpness, contrast, and tone if necessary.
- You have the option to save the photo in the size and style you want after you are satisfied with it.

Lightroom Classic's Dodge and Burn tools let you enhance your black-and-white photos' tonal range and highlight certain areas. Experiment with the tools, and bear in mind that subtlety is frequently the key to success.

CHAPTER 8

BLACK AND WHITE PHOTOGRAPHY

Expertise and intuition are required for editing monochrome footage. A few basic black-and-white editing tricks may help your work stand out.

No matter how dramatic or understated your picture edits are going to be, these tips will help you maximize your time while working in black and white.

Choose the Right Editing Software

Before we get into post-processing, let's examine several popular editing programs and plug-ins. There is specialized software that caters to the needs of digital photographers. Make sure you're comfortable with using a few programs before you go into black-and-white photography.

To a certain extent, several of these serve as general-purpose editors. There are specialized ones that cater to black and white photographers, providing them with more options.

After you decide on an editor, there's no turning back. Most of these sites include free trials, so you can test out several options before you buy.

Adobe Lightroom & Photoshop

With Lightroom and Photoshop's extensive toolkit, you can enhance color and black-and-white images alike. Lightroom has a variety of tools and modification brushes that can lift the mood of any photo.

Photoshop offers an extensive set of editing tools that are ideal for a wide variety of creative projects, including repainting. To convert your photographs to black and white and make them seem amazing, you just need one adjustment layer.

Adobe Camera RAW

You can open RAW files using Adobe Camera RAW. Use this program to easily convert and edit your RAW photographs if that's what you usually shoot in.

Those who often work with RAW files and need to convert or edit them may find this program valuable, not only for black and white photographers.

Nik Silver Efex

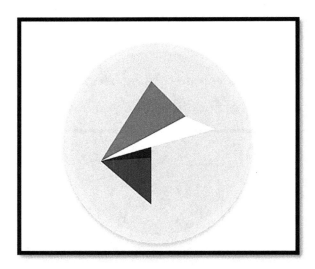

For photographers working in black and white who like to have creative control, DxO offers the Nik Silver Efex plug-in. Those familiar with Adobe Photoshop and Lightroom will find this to be an excellent option. In these apps, you may find tools that do nothing but edit pictures.

Among the many customization options provided by the plugin are Structure, Amplify Blacks, and Dynamic Brightness. If you are looking for a comprehensive editing experience, this plug-in might be a solid pick.

Exposure X7

You can use Exposure X7 either independently or as an add-on for Photoshop or Lightroom. Similar to the first two, this application caters to a wide range of photographers and offers a variety of capabilities for black-and-white images.

What sets this program apart are the editing effects and layers it offers. You can apply creative blur and texture to your black-and-white photographs to make them seem more fashionable.

Editing Black and White Photos

You can begin editing your photos in the Develop module once you've shared them.

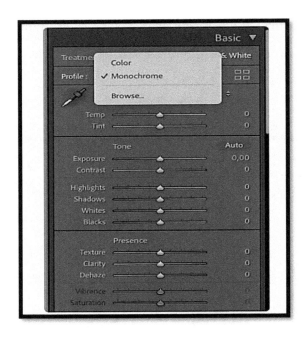

Convert to Black and White

If you are working with color pictures, you need to convert them to black and white. There are 4 ways to go about this:

- **Use a saturation slider**. Move to -100 on the saturation. Be aware that after this, you will not have many options for changes. This is a good option if you just want to apply a few minor adjustments to your images before converting them to black and white.

- In the Basic panel, right next to Color, you should see the **Black & White** option; click on it. Additional editing options will be available to you going forward.

- Select **Monochrome** on the **Basic Panel** by clicking on **Color**, located next to Profile.

- You should use black-and-white filters. This type of filter is termed a preset in Lightroom and an action in Photoshop CC. Filters make it simple to add a chic black-and-white effect to your photos.

Use Adjustment Sliders

Using the saturation slider to convert your images to black and white could make you realize that something is absent. If no adjustments are made, a black-and-white photograph may not appear as captivating or vibrant as its color version.

Changing the black and white tones is a simple way to address this with the use of adjustment sliders. When working with black and white, these parameters are crucial. The color sliders in Lightroom can be found under the B&W panel. This panel will be invisible when the Saturation scale is set to -100.

In your black-and-white photos, shifting the bars to the left will make some hues darker. As you drag them to the right, the corresponding hues will lighten. Enhancing the shadows with greater contrast and depth is a great method to improve the overall appearance of your images.

A ladybug curled up on a leaf is depicted in the black-and-white photograph above. The red and green sliders can be adjusted to make the colors more noticeable. The ladybug's color will darken as the leaf's color will lighten. To get lighter bugs and darker leaves, flip it over and try it that way. Shooting style is a factor.

Create Contrast

After you finish editing your black-and-white image, head to the Basic panel. The tools in this panel allow you to make tiny adjustments to your photo.

For your black-and-white photograph to stand out, you must add contrast. To achieve this, simply drag the contrast slider to the right. If you manage to pull this off underhandedly, it will be fascinating.

Another way to increase contrast is to darken the blacks and brighten the highlights. Underneath the Basic panel, you'll find the Tone Curve tool, which you can use to further adjust your image.

Differentiate Between Texture, Clarity, and Dehaze

The dehaze, clarity, and texture tools can dramatically improve your black-and-white photos. They are similar in function, but distinct in other respects.

- **Texture:** You can make your images' varying degrees of detail stand out more with the help of texture. Unlike the Details panel's sharpening tool, it will not introduce noise into your black-and-white images. The 3D effect will be rendered with utmost clarity.

- **Clarity:** In terms of clarity, the midtones are the only ones that stand out. In this way, you can get a balanced and clear appearance in images that lack depth.

- **Dehaze:** If your image does not have deep enough shadows, try using the dehaze slider. Fog, haze, or smoke in black-and-white landscape photography might be the culprit here. Simply dragging the tool to the right will eliminate the haze from your photographs.

  You can get all of these outcomes by dragging the bars to the right. If you move them to the left, the result will be the inverse.

To achieve the effect of soft black-and-white images, shift the texture or clarity slider to the left. Shift the dehaze slider to the left to achieve a foggy effect in your photos.

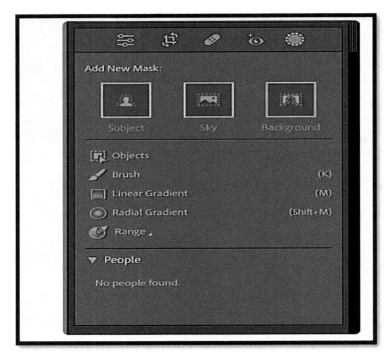

Use a Brush to Make Selective Edits

What if you simply want the focus on your primary idea to stand out? What if you'd like to highlight the model's eyes but don't want to alter the rest of the image? You can highlight a specific area of your monochrome image with the masking tool.

In the **Develop module**, directly above the **Basic panel,** you'll see a collection of five icons. The last icon is a circle with dots surrounding it; click on that, press **Brush**. To adjust the brush size, use the buttons located at the panel's top. It is recommended to set the feather to 100. When you put this on, your brush will have a softer edge, which will make the cuts you choose appear more natural.

The sliders in your photo can be customized to your liking. To make specific areas of your image stand out, drag the highlights tool to the right. If you want your model's eyes to stand out more, you can adjust the texture and sharpness levels.

After that, you can make the changes you like by using a brush. To adjust the level of intensity, simply reposition the buttons. Press the circle button once more to dismiss the brush panel.

Create an Atmosphere Using Colors

After you're satisfied with all the edits, you can shift your focus to creating an atmosphere in your image. You can experiment with various color effects or blur your photographs.

Although this step is not necessary, it might assist you in creating a distinct style as a black-and-white shooter.

By descending the page, you can access the Color Grading panel. Midtones, shadows, and highlights can all be colored in this area. Just by dragging the circle in the center of the wheel, you can change the color. As you go further from the center of the circle, the color impact becomes brighter.

If you're going for a minimalist style, just a touch of color will help the black and white blend together. Color grading typically makes black-and-white photos appear older. While the outcome is intriguing, it may not complement all aesthetic preferences.

Common Black and White Photography Editing Mistakes

When working on a black-and-white image, it's easy to go overboard with the editing. The common error that people make when editing black-and-white images is to apply too much processing.

When editing your black-and-white images, be sure you don't commit these blunders. They will simplify everything and guarantee stunning results every time.

Editing JPEG Files

No need to do this on filming day. While JPEG files are tiny, they do not provide as much editing flexibility.

However, there is no compression in RAW files, therefore they are larger. After you alter them, you'll have greater creative flexibility.

If you're not able to shoot in RAW, it's okay. Whenever you get the opportunity, invest in equipment that can capture RAW files for better results. Your workflow will drastically alter the next time you get the opportunity to edit raw black-and-white images!

Too Much Contrast

Every black-and-white photo requires a unique degree of retouching. If your black and white images are quite muted and have a lot of gray regions, you may choose to adjust the contrast slider to its farthest right. That usually results in less-than-ideal photos.

Increasing contrast is easy using Lightroom's many tools. Beautiful black-and-white highlights may be created with the highlights and whites tools. The blacks and shadows options allow you to create completely black shadows.

Assuming you know what you're doing, these editing tools can completely transform your image.

Too Much Clarity or Texture

An effective black-and-white photograph may be enhanced by adding depth and clarity. Be careful when you utilize them as they can alter your picture. It may be difficult to see if your black-and-white image is off-kilter if you gently shift the scales to the right.

To avoid making changes that are too substantial, make it a practice to repeatedly use the same tool to make little adjustments. Unless you're going for that appearance, set the bar back to zero if you're not satisfied. Make minor adjustments to the original if you think the second one looks better.

Using Presets for Black and White Photography

1. **Select a photo to change to black and white**

   Select a color image from the Library module grid. To open the chosen picture in the Develop module, click **Develop** in the Module Picker at the top of the screen or press the **D** key.

2. **Apply a black-and-white preset**

We will examine ways to modify the black-and-white treatment once we have used a preset to turn the picture to black and white. The Presets panel can be accessed by clicking on its title bar, located on the left side of the Develop module. In the Presets panel, you can access a variety of black-and-white presets by clicking on the B&W region.

When you hover your cursor over the black-and-white presets, a preview of how each one will appear in your photo will be displayed. Select a preset from this section of the image by clicking on it. I decided on **B&W High Contrast** for this particular situation. You may apply a new preset on top of this one if you change your mind, or you can click the **Reset** option to return to the initial photo and apply a new preset there.

3. **Open the Basic panel**

Now that a pre-set black-and-white effect has been applied, let's examine how the effect can be adjusted for a given photo. Access the Basic adjustment panel by navigating to the Develop module's right side. It is evident that we utilized a black-and-white image in the settings and increased the contrast by using the Whites and Blacks sliders.

4. **Customize with manual adjustments**

This photo appears to be very bright even now. Adjust the Exposure slider in the Basic panel to around -0.60 to slightly darken the image. Raising the Clarity scale to around +25 will make the image pop more. The midtones will be more contrasty as a result of this.

5. **Adjust the black-and-white mix**

    You can use the sliders in the black-and-white panel to vary the way the original picture's colors are converted to black and white.

    Note: Please be aware that in Lightroom Classic, the Black & White panel cannot be accessed until a photo has been black and white-edited.

    This panel allows you to adjust the grayscale brightness of each color in the original image. Set the Blue scale to around -20 to reduce the perceived blueness of the sky and water. You can adjust the brightness of the lifeguard tower's black bars by dragging the red scale.

To achieve the precise black-and-white effect you like, you can use the many presets or make personal adjustments.

CHAPTER 9

HDR AND PANORAMA MERGING

Creating HDR Images

Bracketing is the process utilized to create HDR images. Combining many images taken at different exposures into one picture allows for a more accurate and comprehensive depiction of the highlights, midtones, and shadows. Since it may be challenging to capture details in both the shadows and the highlights with only natural light, this technique is popular among landscape photographers.

Landscape photography is another excellent subject for HDR processing due to the requirement for extremely motionless settings. Because of the stacking nature of the photos in bracketing, a minimum of three almost identical photographs except for exposure are required for the procedure. This becomes more challenging when dealing with dynamic objects, such as living beings. To guarantee consistent shots, a tripod is a must-have accessory.

Once you have all of the images in Lightroom, you can merge them. The desired result may be achieved by experimenting with various merging parameters.

Step 1: Select the Bracketed Images

Before beginning the HDR merging, decide which images will be utilized. You get to decide which of the images in brackets to use. All of these might be useful for you. Later on, I will elaborate on that. After you've decided on the images to use, be sure to choose each one. This is something you can accomplish in the Develop or Library modules.

Step 2: Photo Merge > HDR

Pick out the images you wish to merge, and then head to **Photo > Photo join > HDR**. Another option is to choose many images, right-click on one of them, and then select

Photo Merge > HDR. On a computer, hit **Ctrl+H** to perform this fast. A window called the HDR Merge Preview will popup. Before you complete the merging, this window will display a preview of the combined files and provide you with three main alternatives.

Remember that the example image may not appear drastically different from some of the initial bracketed images. It will appear flat. The intended result is that way because processing is still required on the final combined image, which is still RAW data.

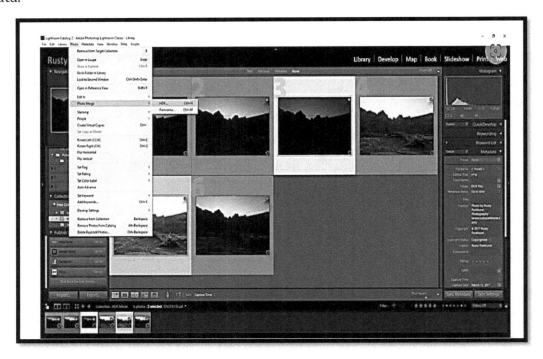

Step 3: Choosing HDR Options

Before the final join, you will see three primary options on the right side of the HDR join Preview window.

- **Auto Align:** Selecting Auto Align causes Lightroom to attempt to align images that were moved between shots; it accomplishes a respectable job of it. With a tripod, this option can be superfluous.

- **Auto Tone:** When you select Auto Tone, a few simple tonal adjustments will be applied to the combined preview image. The picture's highlights will probably be lowered, its shadows raised, and its white and black points adjusted. This gives you a better idea of the tonal range and helps the image seem more balanced. Similar to Lightroom's Auto button in the Develop Module's Basic Panel, the HDR sample window's Auto Tone button is also identical. Usually, I just leave this choice unchecked as the final adjustment is going to be done later. Additionally, the HDR look it imparts is something I'm not a fan of, so I disable it while taking pictures.

- **Deghost Amount:** This adjustment eliminates or significantly reduces **ghosting**, the effect that occurs when objects in a scene move around in between shots. Decaying is the process of replacing pixels from the original image with new ones after they have shifted between frames. Anything in motion, like clouds, automobiles, or plants, can benefit from this. You should pick for greater deghosting as the amount of movement increases. Selecting the **Show Deghost Overlay** checkbox will reveal the concealed areas of the image. In the absence of any movable objects in the images, selecting **None** is the obvious choice. Then, for optimal image quality, lower it to the lowest possible level.

It's important to know that the HDR settings will stay the same the next time you use Photo Merge. Depending on the image, the options you need to activate each time may be different.

The HDR Merge Preview window. Note the HDR Options on the right side.

The image has an HDR look because Auto Tone is selected in the HDR Merge Preview window.

The Deghosting option is useful for masking movements between frames. Selecting **Show Deghost Overlay** will reveal the areas that have been marked with masking.

Step 4: Merging the Images

To finalize the photo, click the Merge button when you're satisfied with the preview. After the selected options have been applied to the image files, the Lightroom filmstrip will be updated to include the merged final product. What you get is an Adobe DNG file, which is a raw file format with 16 bits of data. Because the combined image preserves all of the source images' raw data, you have a lot of leeway to manipulate the final product.

On top are the images with the lightest and darkest brackets. You can see the combined image at the bottom before you make any adjustments.

The picture that was joined in Lightroom's Develop Module. In the Basic Panel, the Auto Tone button has been chosen.

Step 5: Edit the Image

The good times are about to begin. The bulk of the work has been performed by the machine up to this point. At this point, you are free to express your creativity by making any necessary adjustments to the final composite image. By adjusting the sliders in Lightroom, you can bring out much more detail in the image. Previously, the brightness scale could only range from -5 to +5 stops; however, this is no longer the case. You can restore information in the lighter regions by using the highlights slider, and you can make the darkest sections much brighter by adjusting the shadows slider. Use the defaults or make your adjustments; the choice is yours. Just as with all of Lightroom's other editing features, these adjustments will not negatively impact the original image. You have the option to undo or start again whenever you choose.

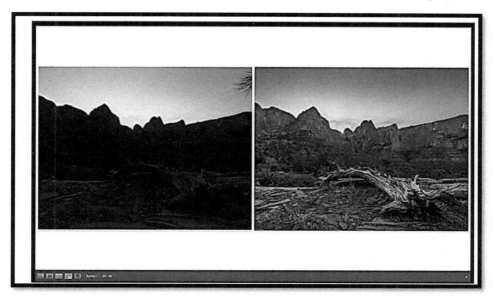

Tips for best results

It's not hard to utilize Lightroom's HDR merging feature. From importing an image to creating the finished image, all it takes are four simple steps. To get the most out of it and make it go even faster, though, there are a few things you can do.

Tip 1: Shoot in RAW

This piece of advice applies to nearly any type of shooting, albeit it may sound repetitive. It is much easier to restore features in the shadows and highlights when shooting in RAW since all of the image data is preserved. Using the RAW file format is crucial. My recommendation is that you utilize it by default. In a pinch, shooting in

JPEG will do. After you finish shooting, make sure you return the camera to RAW mode.

Tip 2: Use only what you need

You can find this to be the case with any number of bracketed photos—three, five, seven, or even nine. To create the HDR, you may not require all of them. To discover what works best for you, you'll need to give a few other approaches a shot. Just use the two images: one with a two-stop less exposure and one with a two-stop more exposure. This could be all that's needed to expedite the merger and acquire what you desire.

Tip 3: Edit after the merge

Avoid making any changes to the images within the brackets before merging them. The photo adjustments made before the merging process will be lost thereafter. You can customize your lens settings before you join, and they will be preserved. Make sure to save any additional edits until you have the final, combined image.

Tip 4: Stack bracketed images

Even if this advice doesn't improve your HDR-making skills, it will help you arrange your photos more effectively. When things are more organized, workflow speeds up. So, more efficient implies quicker. Quicker progress is preferred. Keeping track of all the bracketed photographs and figuring out which ones match with what might be a challenge when you have a card full of photos. To make things more organized and simpler to deal with, stack each set of bracketed images on top of the other.

You should begin by importing all of the images into Lightroom. **Photo > Stacking > Auto-Stack by Capture Time** is what you need to do. Time is of the essence for your tasks. You can adjust the intervals between stacks in the resulting pop-up window. This is based on the premise that each pair of bracketed photos can be captured quickly. For nighttime photographs, I recommend a shutter speed of 10 seconds. For greater shutter speeds, such as those used for night shots, this time setting would have to be significantly longer. Press the **Stack** button when the moment is ripe.

Lightroom will determine which images should be combined based on their time stamps. To access **Stacking > Collapse all Stacks**, either return to the Photo Menu or right-click on any photo. All the photo sets that fall within the specified period will be stacked. In the upper left corner of a picture, which resembles a stack of white boxes, there is a little white box. You can determine the picture is a stack by looking at this box. You can tell how many photographs are in the stack by looking at the number in the box. You may increase or decrease the size of each layer whenever you choose.

The Stacking feature in the Photo Menu. Do this within Lightroom's Library Module.

You can configure the time interval between stacks in Auto-Stacking.

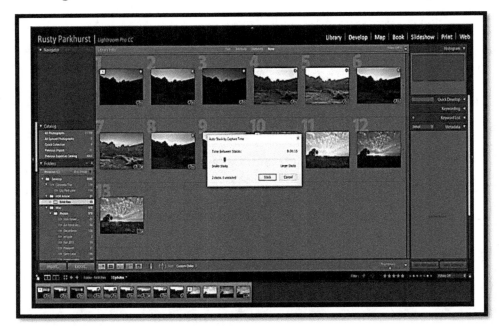

Tip 5: Reset HDR options

When I talked about Step 3, the HDR settings from the previous session will be retained the next time Photo Merge is launched. After the HDR merging is complete, select two images and reopen the preview window. You can stop creating new HDR images by deselecting all of the options and then clicking **Cancel**. You can learn to utilize tools more effectively with this simple and fast technique.

Tip 6: Skip the preview

Time appears to be an elusive commodity for me. In no way. However, I am fully supportive of any measure that might expedite the process. Editing my images is an artistic experience that I enjoy. There are a few workarounds for the HDR viewing window. Holding down Shift when selecting Photo Merge > HDR allows the merging to run in the background, allowing you to multitask.

On a computer, you can achieve the same result by selecting the images you wish to merge, and then hitting **Ctrl+Shift+H**. When you utilize these techniques, you won't get any samples. However, if you adjusted the HDR settings as mentioned in the previous advice, the scene was rather static, and the photographs were shot on a stand, you won't require a preview. If you find that anything is amiss during the merging, you can easily revert to using the sample.

Create a Panorama

Panorama Photo Merge

Select the images you wish to combine into a panorama. You won't need to modify the final product because it will be a RAW DNG file, which allows you to make edits once stitching is complete. With Lightroom's built-in **Photo Merge** feature, you can easily combine many photographs into one. It can stitch together landscapes and create HDR photos. Naturally, the panorama feature will be our primary area of attention. Select the images you like to merge with the right mouse button and then choose **Photo Merge > Panorama... or Photo > Photo Merge > Panorama...** from the Lightroom menu. This will launch the tool. Pressing **CTRL + M** (or **CMD + M** on a Mac) is another quick way to access the tool.

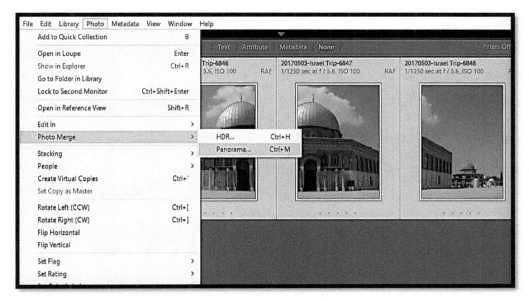

147

This will open the Panorama Merge Preview, which will look like this:

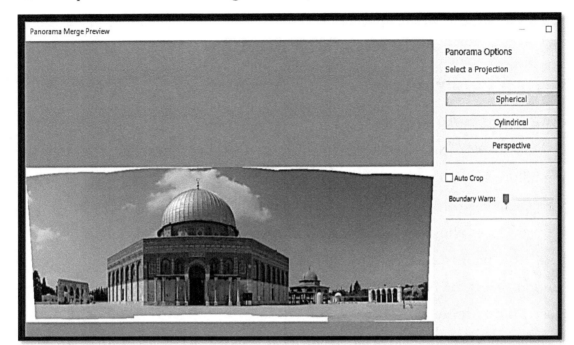

The Panorama Merge tool is rather simple, with only a handful of options, as compared to certain third-party tools. This makes it an excellent choice for beginners in the field of picture stitching. One can choose between spherical, cylindrical, or perspective panorama projection. Two more styles are available: **Auto Crop** and **Boundary Warp**. Let's have a closer look at each apparatus.

Panorama Projections

The default is circular, which is reasonable given that the majority of your Lightroom photographs will be circular. On the other hand, how do perspective, spherical, and cylindrical perspectives differ from one another? Check it out:

- **Spherical Projection**: Most projections use spherical projections. The effect is to make the mapped pictures appear to be inside a sphere. Wide and multi-row photos are made easy using this tool. Since it doesn't stretch anything, the spherical warp typically produces the most realistic effect when photographing close things. Take a look at this hand-held photo I shot in Jerusalem of the Dome of the Rock:

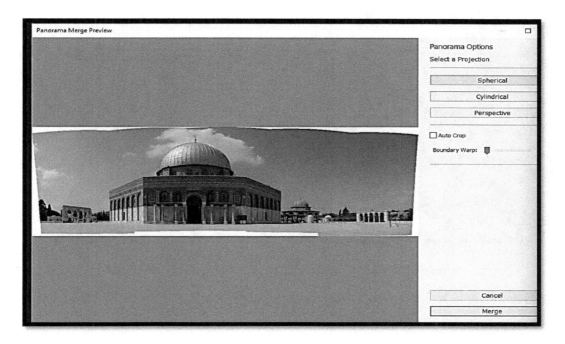

Though somewhat distorted, the resulting image appears realistic, as one would expect from an object at the same distance.

- **Cylindrical Projection:** For example, you can use cylindrical projection to make your images appear as though they were mapped to a cylinder's interior. It's great for broad shots, but watch out: it will attempt to maintain perfectly straight vertical lines, which may severely distort your objects. Examine the resulting shift in the building's profile using the same panoramic images:

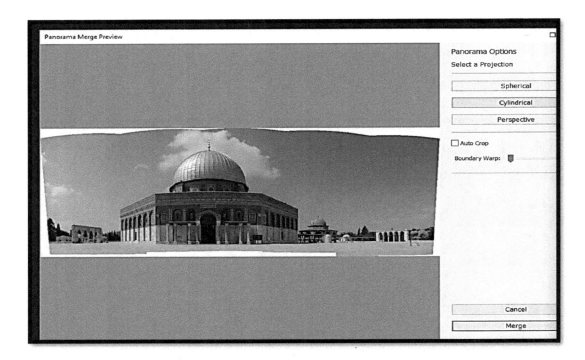

The roof appears to be stretched too far; it conceals the reality. Because the technique has the potential to artificially inflate the landscape, I do not recommend using Cylindrical Projection on landscape photographs. Exercise caution when utilizing it.

- **Perspective Projection:** When photographing buildings, particularly those with several stories, the Perspective Projection mode is ideal for capturing the subject from all angles. Because of the potential for distorted edge lines when shooting at shorter focal lengths, wide horizontal building panoramas can be challenging to use. In Perspective Projection, examine the scene's background:

Lines may not remain straight in your photo if it's like the one up there; this is particularly true at the frame's corners. The structure itself is sturdy, but the surrounding area appears to be in disrepair. However, there are instances where the Perspective Projection is the sole option available, such as when you wish to see continuously rising and falling structures. Take a look at the spherical projection image below, created from four vertical shots:

The clock tower stands out because of its unusual design, which makes the upper part of the structure appear curved and larger than the lower part. The issue disappears and the structure takes on a more realistic appearance when you use Perspective Projection.

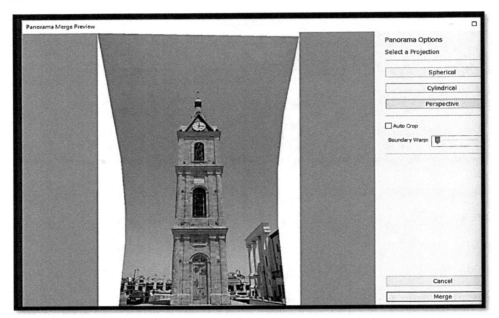

I recommend experimenting with the various projection methods to find the one that suits each panorama photo the best. Even though all three of these projector methods are compatible with panoramas, certain panoramas are only compatible with one. For the most lifelike results, spherical projection is my go-to method. However, as seen before, Cylindrical and Perspective views are more appropriate in some situations.

Auto Crop

The majority of panoramas require image stretching to accommodate the various projection formats, as seen in the aforementioned examples, leaving blank space around the borders of the frame. To fill in the blanks, just use the **Auto Crop** feature; it will detect where there are gaps and crop the image accordingly. Using Spherical Projection with the Auto Crop option enabled, have a look at the image below:

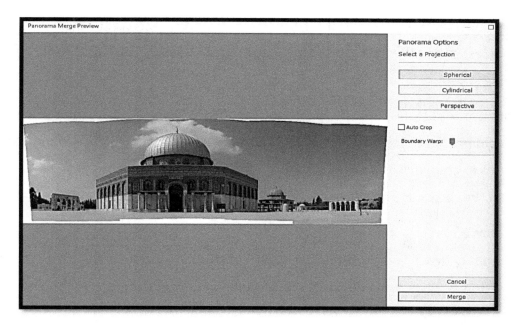

Right away, Lightroom adjusted the image to eliminate the white borders. So, I can skip the step of cropping the image in Lightroom and get right to editing.

Although AutoCrop is a great tool, you shouldn't always use it because it could remove too much of the image. When stitching a large panorama, if one area is noticeably poorer than the others, you will significantly diminish the overall image quality. In some cases, manually cropping the images may be the best option to prevent excessive clipping.

The proximity of the dome's peak to the picture's edge is something I find unappealing. There was an excessive amount of vacant space on the far-right side of the image in comparison to the middle. To save some space at the top of the frame, I may remove the image on the right side of the screen in this instance.

Boundary Warp

The Boundary Warp feature is fairly new to Lightroom (it's only in Lightroom CC right now), although it is a much-needed addition to the program. To fill the area and achieve, it distorts the entire picture. To retain most of the image and reduce the impact of Auto Crop, the border warp function can be quite useful in cases when lines or a horizon are not well defined. Keeping with the previous example, let's examine the Dome of the Rock image while increasing the Boundary Warp to 100%:

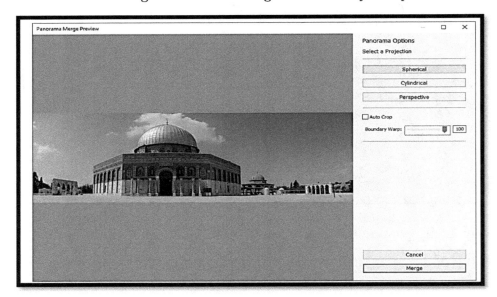

Because the image is extended to the boundaries of the frame when the setting is set to 100%, Auto Crop is unnecessary. While I can see how using this feature at 100%

would work in certain panoramas, I find that it overstretches the lines in most panoramas.

This photo clearly shows that the skyline isn't perfectly straight; in fact, it seems somewhat crooked on both the left and right edges of the frame. It would be wise to examine each image independently in this instance. With Auto Crop enabled, I discovered that 70 was the optimal border warp number for the image up top.

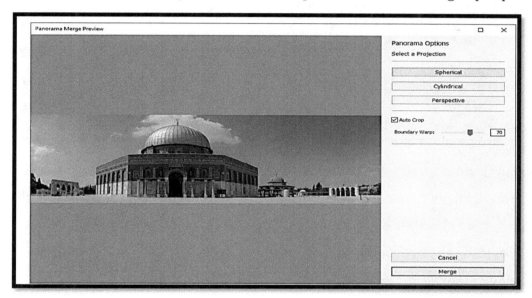

Because it provides me with additional breathing space at the top of the photo, this is the version I would want to work with. I would have liked a little more sky in the final product, and the fact that the cloud is cropped makes me unhappy. Next, we'll go over how to create a two-row photo because I was unable to zoom out or return to the field.

Stitching Multiple-Row Panoramas

Any panorama with more than two rows is called a multi-row panorama. For high-resolution images or to capture more of the scene than your focal length permits, this is a lifesaver. I created a two-row image of the Dome of the Rock, as you can see below:

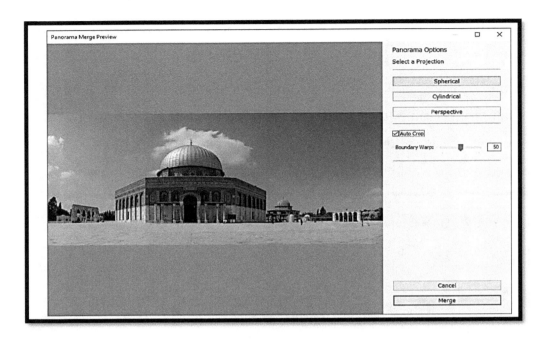

Lightroom did a good job of stitching together the eight images. Both the top and bottom rows have four items each. A high-resolution image larger than a single-row panoramic was in my possession before I realized it. However, stitching it took some time. You can see how shooting in many rows may be useful in some situations, even if I removed the background and some sky from the final image.

So far, I have done a lot of work in Lightroom creating landscapes with several rows. For the most part, I stick to two-row landscapes since I find that they provide more room for detail. The more rows you have, though, the more difficult it will be to stitch landscapes. Lightroom may have memory and resource limitations that prevent it from stitching more than two rows. I usually stick to two rows, although I've dabbled with three-row landscapes before, and the outcomes were all over the place.

Finishing Up in Photoshop

Lightroom performs an excellent job at panoramic joining for the most part, but occasionally you'll have to import the panorama into Photoshop to correct distortions and issues with joining. Although it's not often, occasionally you may see minor parallax errors, excessive bending that needs correction, or topics that require duplication. It was obvious that the image was distorted after Lightroom finished assembling the above photo of the Dome of the Rock. It seems like the lines are distorted in areas where it doesn't make sense. I imported the picture into Photoshop and used the Warp tool to correct the crooked lines.

After I finished editing it in Photoshop, the final product looked like this:

For a more compact design, I leveled off the sky, amplified the contrast, and further cropped the image (click to expand). A 133 by 54-inch piece of paper may hold an image with a resolution of 150 dpi since the final product is around 20,000 pixels wide and 8200 pixels high.

CHAPTER 10

WORKING WITH LOCAL ADJUSTMENTS (GRADUATED FILTER, BRUSH, RADIAL FILTER)

The adjustment panels in the Develop module allow you to tweak the color and tone of a whole picture. But there are instances when a complete overhaul isn't necessary. A certain area of an image needs your attention. To bring out more detail in a portrait or enhance the blue sky in a landscape, you may choose to brighten the subject's face. To perform local modifications in Lightroom Classic, you can utilize the Adjustment Brush tool or the Graduated Filter tool. Colors and tones can be changed with their help.

You can carefully apply Exposure, Clarity, Brightness, and other adjustments to photos by **painting** them on with the Adjustment Brush tool.

The Graduated Filter tool allows you to subtly alter the picture's tones, including exposure and clarity, across a specific region. Whether the space is wide or narrow is up to you.

Adjustments done locally in Lightroom Classic's Develop module are temporary and, like all other adjustments, do not alter the original image.

Apply an adjustment brush or filter effect

1. Press D to access the Develop module after selecting an image to edit in the Library module. To switch to a different image on the Filmstrip or Collections panel, you can do so in the Develop module.

2. You can access the Adjustment Brush tool and Graduated Filter tool in the Develop module's tool strip, respectively.

3. From the Effect pop-up menu, choose the type of change you want to make or drag the sliders:

    Temp: You can modify the color temperature of a specific area of the image to make it warmer or cooler. Graded filter temperature effects can improve the quality of photos shot in a variety of lighting conditions.

    Tint: Makes up for a green or magenta color cast.

    Exposure: Changes the overall brightness of the image. Dodging and burning effects can be achieved with an exposure local adjustment.

    Contrast: Modifies the picture's contrast, which mostly impacts the midtones.

    Highlights: Revives underexposed or overexposed areas of a picture's detail.

    Shadows: Revives lost detail in an image's too-dark shadow areas.

    Whites: Alters the appearance of a picture's white points.

    Blacks: Alters the appearance of a picture's black points.

    Texture: Adjusts the degree to which textured areas of your shot stand out or blend. Shift the slider to the left to smooth out features. To make them stand out more, tilt it to the right. Changing the Texture option does not affect the color or tone.

Clarity: Increases local contrast to make a scene seem more three-dimensional.

Dehaze: Reduces or increases the amount of haze in an image.

Hue: Hue alters the color of an image. To get precise adjustments, select **Use Fine Adjustment.**

Saturation: Modifies the intensity of a color.

Sharpness: Enhances the picture's sharpness by bringing out the edges. With a negative value, fine details become blurry.

Noise: When dark regions are opened up, luminance noise becomes less noticeable.

Moiré: Gets rid of color aliasing, which is another name for moiré effects.

Defringe: Removes colors from the ends of the fringe.

Color: Adds a color to the area that needs to be fixed locally. To select a color, click on the color swatch. The color effect will still be there even after converting the image to black and white.

Other effects: Extra effects can be applied to particular activities, such as enhancing irises, softening skin tone, or whitening teeth.

Note: If you're using Mac OS X, go to **Lightroom Classic > Preferences** to locate Burn (Darken), Dodge (Lighten), Iris Enhance, Soften Skin, and Teeth Whitening. If you're using Windows, go to **Edit > Preferences**. The **Presets** panel has a button labeled **Restore Local Adjustment Presets**. Press this button.

4. By sliding the sliders for each effect, you can adjust the numbers.

5. Choose choices for Adjustment Brush A (Only for the Adjustment Brush tool):

Size: The size of the brush tip is indicated in pixels via the size property.

Feather: Smoothly transitions between the brushed region and the pixels surrounding it. The brush's ability to demonstrate the quantity of feathers is shown by the distance between the inner and outer circles.

Flow: Controls the rate at which the adjustment is implemented.

Auto Mask: Limits brush strokes to areas that are the same color.

Density: The clarity of the stroke is determined by this attribute.

6. Simply drag the image inside the effect to apply it.

Mask mode changes to Edit when a pin⊙ appears at the initial application point. The center, low, and high levels of a Graduated Filter effect are depicted by three white lines.

Modify a Graduated Filter or Radial Filter using brush controls

To modify Graduated Filter masks, you can adjust the brush settings. Click the Brush button next to New/Edit to access the brush settings after applying a mask.

In contexts where they make sense, use the plus (+) and minus (-) brushes. A, B, and Erase are the three filter brushes available in Lightroom Classic. The following parameters are adjustable for these instruments:

- **Size:** How big the brush is.
- **Feather:** The quantity of feathering for the brush.

- **Flow:** The quantity of paint applied to the surface with each stroke is called the flow. As an illustration, when the Flow is set to 20%, the initial stroke is enhanced with 20% paint strength. With the next stroke, the paint's strength is increased to 40%.

- **Density:** The thickest layer of paint that the brush can cover. To illustrate, with this parameter set to 40%, the brush will not be able to paint objects with an opaqueness greater than 40%.

Keep in mind that you can paint inside an area's edges by using the AutoMask feature. By obscuring the region, Lightroom Classic prevents your brushstrokes from going beyond it. Before painting, position the tip of the brush precisely inside the desired region.

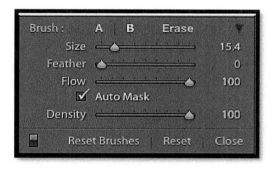

After you've finished modifying the A, B, and Erase brushes, hit **Reset Brushes** to undo everything you've done.

Edit an Adjustment Brush or Graduated Filter/Radial Filter effect

To modify the impact of a Graduated Filter or Adjustment Brush, you can perform any of the following:

- To make the pin and Graduated Filter guides visible or invisible, hit the **H** key. Another option for selecting the display mode is the Show Edit Pins menu located in the toolbar.

- Press **O** on the Adjustment Brush tool to show or hide a mask overlay. Additionally, you have the option to Show Selected Mask Overlay in the toolbar.

- To toggle between various effects using the Adjustment Brush tool with a red, green, or white mask, press **Shift+O**.

- The Effects sliders need to be moved.

- To roll back the modifications you made, use **Ctrl+Z** on a Windows computer or **Command+Z** on a Mac.

- Click **Reset** to remove all your modifications to the selected tool.

- Press the **Delete** key to remove an Adjustment Brush or Graduated Filter effect after selecting its pin.

- Drag With the Adjustment Brush tool, move the pointer over the pin and drag the arrow with two points to the right to make the effect stronger or to the left to weaken it.

- Use the Erase brush option and paint over the adjustment using the Adjustment Brush tool to delete a portion of the adjustment.

- To move the effect's center, use the Graduated Filter tool and drag the pin.

- For Graduated Filter tool, move the mouse over the white line in the middle until a bent, two-pointed arrow appears. Then, drag to turn the effect.

- Using the Graduated Filter tool, drag a thin white line to the picture's edge to amplify the effect at the extremes. Effects at the extremes of the range become less noticeable as the mouse moves in the direction of the picture's center.

Advanced retouching techniques

For those looking for more sophisticated editing options in Lightroom Classic, here they are:

1. **Spot Removal Tool** : Dust spots and other minor imperfections may be easily removed with the help of the Spot Removal tool. As for more intricate editing tasks:

    o Utilize the **Clone** mode to copy a clean area over a flaw.

    o To get a more harmonious blend of textures and tones, switch to the Heal mode.

    o To get precise control, adjust the size of the brush and the quantity of feathering.

2. **Graduated and Radial Filters for Dodge and Burn:** Dodging and burning can be fine-tuned with the use of graduated and radial filters, which allow you to make exact adjustments to brightness and darkness, respectively:

    o To make specific areas of your images darker or brighter, apply a graduated filter.

    o To highlight a certain topic, use a Radial Filter to adjust the picture's exposure or contrast.

3. **Adjustment Brush for Localized Adjustments:** You can use the Adjustment Brush to make localized adjustments to certain areas of your image. For example:

    o You can change the exposure, clarity, and sharpness for retouching skin.

    o Enhance the appearance of your eyes by adjusting their brightness, clarity, or color.

    o To alter the hue, clarity, or amount of background noise, simply paint over specific regions.

4. **Advanced Color Grading:** When you go to the Develop module's Color Grading panel, you'll see options for more sophisticated color correction and tone adjustments:
   o   Separately adjust the shadow, mid-tone, and highlight color balances.
   o   To spice up color grading, use the Split Toning panel to apply contrasting hues to the highlights and shadows.

5. **HSL/Color Panel for Color Adjustments:** More control over each color is available in the HSL/color panel, which is used for color adjustments.
   o   Modify the brightness, saturation, and hue of certain colors in your image.
   o   If you want to change skin tone or make certain colors less saturated or brighter, this is going to be your best bet.

6. **Use the Dehaze Slider for Atmospheric Effects:** It's not only for removing haze; the Dehaze slider has other, more dramatic uses as well.
   o   If you want your images to have greater contrast and drama, raise the Dehaze slider.
   o   A dreamy, hazy effect can be achieved by dragging the Dehaze slider to the left.

7. **Create Virtual Copies for Multiple Edits:** Experiment with various fixes without affecting the original by making multiple virtual copies.
   o   Select an image and click **Create Virtual Copy**.
   o   To compare, edit each virtual copy differently.

8. **Enhance Detail with Sharpening and Noise Reduction:** The Detail panel provides access to more advanced tools for these processes:
   o   To make the image crisper, use the sliders for Amount, Radius, and Detail.
   o   Use the Luminance and Color sliders to eliminate noise.

9. **Use the Range Mask for Precise Selections:**

    ○ For minor adjustments made using the Graduated Filter, Radial Filter, or Adjustment Brush, utilize the Range Mask feature.

    ○ Make more specific color or brightness selections with the help of the Range Mask.

10. **Lens Corrections for Distortion and Chromatic Aberration:** Enhance the image's quality and authenticity by erasing lens defects and chromatic aberration:

    ○ Access the Lens Corrections panel by opening the Develop module. Activate **Enable Profile Corrections** along with **Remove Chromatic Aberration.**

11. **Create Presets for Consistent Edits:**

    ○ After you discover a retouching method that suits you, save your settings as presets. This will allow you to apply the same adjustments to other photographs simultaneously.

Advanced color correction and grading techniques

Lightroom Classic's powerful color correction and grading capabilities necessitate a toolbox full of techniques for nailing the tone, mood, and color balance of your images. Here are a few suggestions for more intricate maneuvers:

1. **Color Grading Panel:** The Color Grading panel is included in the Develop module and allows you to adjust the color balance of your picture. Highlights, midtones, and blacks can be individually adjusted.

    ○ Adjust the Shadows slider to apply a certain color tone to the darker areas.

    ○ To obtain mid-range tones, modify the Midtones setting.

    ○ Simply use the Highlights slider to alter the hue of the more prominent areas.

2. **Split Toning:** Highlights and shadows can be given fascinating color tones with the Split Toning panel.

   o   To make the darker and brighter areas seem different hues, adjust the Highlight Hue and Shadow Hue settings.

   o   Use the Balance slider to alter the ratio of highlights to shadows.

3. **HSL/Color Panel:** Select and edit specific colors in an image using the HSL/Color panel.

   o   To modify the hues' colors, use the Hue sliders.

   o   To make some colors more or less vibrant, adjust the Saturation slider.

   o   To adjust the brightness of each color, use the Luminance option.

4. **Camera Calibration Panel:** You can utilize the Camera Calibration panel for smaller color adjustments.

   o   Moving the sliders labeled Red Primary, Green Primary, and Blue Primary allows you to adjust the color combination to your liking.

5. **Targeted Adjustment Tool:** The Tone Curve and HSL/Color panels each have the Targeted Adjustment Tool.

   o   Select the area you want to modify in terms of color or tone by clicking and dragging the tool icon.

   o   You can precisely modify the colors in your image with it.

6. **Graduated and Radial Filters for Color Grading:** Apply color grading with care by using these filters.

   o   To add drama to the image, apply a gentle blue tint to the sky using a Graduated Filter.

  o Apply a warm glow to a specific region using a Radial Filter to highlight it.

7. **Luminance Range Mask:** Make local adjustments to certain light levels with the help of the Luminance Range Mask.

  o Luminance Range Mask can be used to exclude areas with high levels of light, such as clouds, to alter the sky's saturation.

8. **Color Profiles:** Lightroom Classic's several color profiles may dramatically alter the final product of your shot.

  o Experiment with several profiles in the Develop section until you discover the one that most closely matches your creative concept.

9. **Use Presets for Consistency:** To ensure that all of your photographs have consistent color grading, create and apply presets. Put together a collection of themes that reflect your preferred aesthetic.

10. **Use the Tone Curve for Color Adjustments:** You can do more than simply change tones with the Tone Curve; you can also use it to tweak colors. Altering scene colors is another possible usage.

  o Create an S-curve in the RGB channel to increase color depth and contrast.

11. **Export with Color Space Considerations:** Please keep the target color space in mind when you export your images. When it comes to printing, the wider color gamuts of Adobe RGB and ProPhoto RGB are preferable to sRGB, which is fine for the web and most other purposes.

12. **Soft Proofing:** One way to see your photographs before you print them is via Lightroom's **Soft Proofing** feature. You may use this to make intelligent changes to the colors.

13. **Regularly Calibrate Your Monitor:** To ensure accurate color judgments when editing, regularly calibrate your display.

To discover your style and improve the quality of your images, experiment with these sophisticated color correction and grading techniques. Keep in mind that a combination of your unique ideas and a delicate touch will provide outcomes that are both professional and pleasing to the sight.

How to use the transform panel for perspective correction

Photographs can have distorted or skewed perspectives if the photographer uses the incorrect lens or holds the camera shakily. The most obvious examples of this kind of distortion are those that contain geometric shapes or lines that are straight. Whether you have images that don't seem right whether viewed from a horizontal or vertical perspective, it is simple to fix them by using the Upright option that is located in the Transform panel.

You can select from four different automatic perspective correction settings when you use the Upright feature.

These modes are Auto, Level, Vertical, Full, and Guided. After selecting the Upright option, you can make the alteration even more significant by manually modifying the transform choices that are based on sliders.

Note: Note that before you use the Upright tool 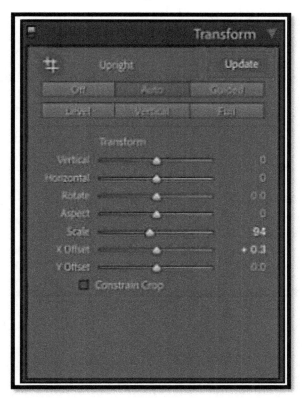 to adjust the perspective, you need first apply lens correction profiles for both your camera and lens. When the lens correction profile is applied first, the picture analysis for upright correction provides a more accurate reflection of the situation.

Ensure that Lens Profile Corrections and Remove Chromatic Aberration are on before adding Upright corrections; this is to ensure that you achieve the best possible results. After making adjustments to the image's upright position, if you apply Lens Corrections, you should use the Update button located in the Transform panel. This will cause Lightroom to examine the image once more and make improvements.

Using Upright modes to correct lens distortion

1. Step into the Develop module and navigate to the Lens Corrections panel. To enable profile corrections, navigate to the Basic tab and click the box that is located next to it.

   Note: It is strongly recommended that you activate lens corrections in the Lens Correction panel before processing the picture with the Upright modes. This is because the lens corrections will be determined by the camera and lens that you are using.

2. Find the box that says **Transform**, and then select one of the five **Upright** options to straighten out the photo.

   Level: Makes corrections to errors that occur in the horizontal plane.

   Vertical: Corrections are made to inaccuracies that occur in the vertical direction.

   Auto: Auto corrects both vertical and horizontal distortions, ensures that the picture is balanced, and preserves as much of the original image as it can.

   Full: Changes in perspective are made simultaneously for full-level, vertical, and auto perspectives.

   Guided: Through the use of this mode, you can alter how the perspective is corrected by drawing two or more lines throughout your shot. To accomplish this:

   1. The Guided Upright tool can be accessed by clicking on it in the upper left corner of the Transform interface. Simply draw the lines on your photo in a straight line.

   2. As soon as you have drawn at least two lines, the picture will undergo an interactive transformation.

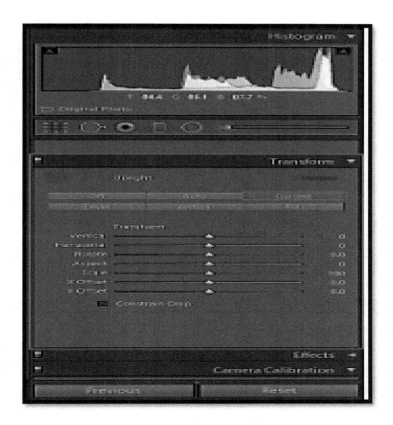

Note:

- When you select the **Upright** option, the crop and any Transform settings that you have previously applied will be reset. While selecting an upright mode, you can maintain those settings by holding down the **Option** key on a Mac or the **Alt** key on a Windows computer.

- To test the five different upright modes, press the Update button located in the upper right corner of the Transform panel whenever you check or uncheck the box that expresses **Enable Profile Corrections**.

3. Make sure to try out all of the different upright modes until you discover the one that suits your needs the most.

    Note: The five Upright modes correct and manage errors in distortion and perspective. For every photograph, the ideal location is going to be different. Explore each of the five settings before deciding which of the five upright modes is the most suitable for your photograph.

    Any time you adjust the perspective of a photograph, you run the risk of getting white patches close to the margins of the picture. To prevent this from occurring, select the Constrain Crop option, which will crop the photo in such a way that it maintains its original dimensions.

4. Besides the options provided by auto-correct, you also can manually alter the perspective of a photograph. Make use of the sliders for X Offset, Y Offset, Rotate, Aspect, Scale, and Vertical Offset to fine-tune the changes in perspective.

Upright Mode shortcuts

Auto, Guided, Level, Vertical, and Full are the many upright modes, and the following are some shortcuts for each of them. If you are working with raw files, employing any of these modes will most likely result in superior results. This is because these modes can use more accurate metadata within the file, such as focal length parameters.

- To transition between the Upright Modes on a Mac or a Windows PC, hit the Control key and the Tab key simultaneously.

- To access the **Guided Upright tool** , press the Shift key in conjunction with the T key. When you drag within the image area, you can add up to four straight lines to each picture. You can move a guide with greater precision (slower movement) by pressing the Option-drag (Mac) or Alt-drag (Win) button simultaneously.

- To activate and deactivate the Guided Upright Loupe, simply press the **O** button.

- The Grid Overlay, located in the toolbar, should be set to **Always** while the **Guided Upright tool** is selected to visually display a reference grid within the image. If the **Grid Overlay** is set to either of those two options, the H key will toggle between the **Never** and **Auto** grid overlay combinations.

- To alter the Tool Overlay settings, use the **A** key. This key allows you to choose between **Always**, **Auto**, and **Never**.

Aspect—If a portion of the image becomes excessively compressed or stretched, the Aspect slider can assist in removing the distortion that has occurred. This is especially helpful in situations where there are humans or animals captured in the photograph.

Revealing Cropped Areas —When you utilize the Upright Modes, the picture that you obtain is frequently cut so that there are no blank places around the edges. This causes the picture to be revealed. To move the image about in the canvas, you can use

175

the sliders labeled Scale, X Offset, or Y Offset. Because of this, you will be able to save significant portions of the original photograph that would otherwise be subject to cropping.

Rotated Crops and Manual Perspective Corrections— It is prohibited to employ rotated crops or manual perspective adjustments on photographs that have already been taken. To make these adjustments, you should instead make use of the Horizontal, Vertical, Rotate, Aspect, Scale, and X/Y Offset controls that are located on the Transform panel.

NOTE: In most cases, these modifications will be detrimental to the upright fixes. As a result of this, selecting one of the Upright modes will reset the crop and manual perspective modifications. This will ensure that the greatest image area that is still usable after an Upright adjustment is displayed.

- To maintain the Crop selections when switching to Upright Mode, press the Option key and click on your Mac or the Alt key and click on your Windows keyboard.

Copy or sync Transform settings

To make it possible for you to utilize it on more than one photo, you can either copy (Copy Settings) or sync (Sync Settings) Upright. Currently, there are three options available to select from both the Copy Settings and Synchronize Settings dialogs. The following are the options:

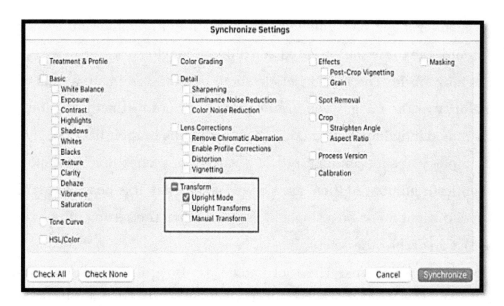

Upright Mode

When the Upright mode is selected, the mode that was selected is copied. On the other hand, the settings are fixed in the photo that they were copied to, and this is determined by the contents of that image.

Upright Transforms

If you select Upright Transforms, the precise Upright change will be replicated and maintained in sync. If you select the box that is located next to the Upright Transforms option, the Upright Mode option will concurrently be selected.

Upright Adjustments

The values that are already set on the Vertical, Horizontal, Rotate, Aspect, Scale, X Offset, and Y Offset buttons are copied when you select Upright Adjustments. They are also copied when you select the Upright Adjustments option.

Choosing when to use the Upright Mode or Upright Transforms options:

When you utilize the Upright modes, each photo is examined and altered according to the information that it contains. Therefore, a photograph that is evaluated in a

177

particular manner might be studied in a slightly different manner if the illumination is different or if the camera is oriented at a different angle.

- **Upright Mode**: The upright mode should be utilized in situations when the majority of the images you are working with are distinct and require to be examined individually to modify them according to their data. To give you an example, you shot photographs of a variety of scenes in a metropolis, but a significant number of them are skewed somewhat. It is possible to utilize the Level Upright mode on a single picture, and then the setting can be replicated across all of the other pictures.

- **Upright Transforms:** The tool known as **Upright Transforms** should be utilized when you have the intention of altering all of the photos in a uniform manner. Consider this scenario: you took multiple photographs of the same location to use them in an HDR process; however, some of the photographs have a tiny tilt to them. It is possible to utilize the Level Upright mode on a photo, and the same adjustments can be made to each of the images that will be used for the HDR image.

How to understand and use split toning

Utilizing split toning in Lightroom is an excellent method for enhancing the color contrast and depth of your photographs. This procedure involves adding a second color to the shadows and highlights of your photo. This color is added to the picture. To accomplish this, open Lightroom and navigate to the Develop module. From there, select the Split Toning option.

Split toning is a technique that allows you to color the highlights and shadows of an image in a distinct manner. This is a technique that was utilized in the laboratory and has been converted into the realm of digital technology. It gives photographers the ability to alter the colors of an image without drastically altering the overall tone of the picture at the same time.

As a result of split toning, the highlights are given a greater amount of color or tone without the blacks being altered, and it also works in the opposite direction. You have the option of simply giving the highlights or the blacks a split tone, or you may do both at the same time.

It is possible to apply the split coloring technique to both color and black-and-white photographs equally. Within a color photograph, the procedure incorporates that tone with the highlights and blacks that are already there in the image.

In the case of a black-and-white photograph, split toning can be utilized to impart a shade of color to the blacks, grays, and whites. This has the potential to appear as a cyanotype or sepia photograph.

The utilization of split tones can be done in a variety of different ways. There are a few standard edits that are performed using this procedure. When you utilize split color, you can alter the white balance of both the shadows and the highlights separately. You don't need to update the entire picture all at once.

The appearance of anything being a movie can also be achieved through the usage of this technology. The goal of split toning is not always to correct something; rather, it is to create something completely original. Filters and themes use a variety of methods, such as split toning, in conjunction with other tools to achieve a certain look.

You can select any hue when you split tone. As a result of the way that certain colors make things appear, some people prefer certain hues more than others.

- **Orange:** Use orange if you want to give a warm glow to your photographs or if you want to correct the white balance. To a large extent, this color is utilized for the highlights.
- **Blue:** Blue can cool down the environment, correct the white balance, or create a cyanotype effect. The most common color chosen is a variety of blues.

- **Brown:** Brown is a color that produces a sepia effect or a softening effect on the colors in the photograph.
- **Teal:** Teal is a color that gives the appearance of a movie.
- **Pinks:** Pinks tend to create a blush appearance.

Using split toning allows you to utilize either one color or two colors. In situations where you are working with two colors, it is ideal to choose colors that complement one another.

The colors that are complementary to one another on the color wheel are called complimentary colors. Orange-blue, red-green, and yellow-purple are some examples of such colors.

When splitting tones, color schemes that are similar to one another can also work nicely. Some examples of color pairs that are displayed adjacent to one another on the color wheel include green-blue and orange-yellow.

When you are working with color in the process of editing images, you should consider working with hues that appear nice on their own. How those colors appear when seen together will likewise look fantastic in a photograph.

Your inspiration can come from the natural world or even from the paint sample department of a hardware store.

Using split toning

In Lightroom, split toning is a simple process to handle. You can make use of a panel in the Develop module that is referred to as split toning.

Not only is it simple to locate, but if you do it on your own, you run the risk of overlooking certain phases and configurations. This is how you can add a split tone to your images in Lightroom.

1. **Open the Image in the Develop Module**

   To view the split toning options, you must first select the image you wish to modify within the Develop panel of Lightroom.

   Initially, make any necessary adjustments to the Basic panel by modifying it as necessary. An example of this would be correcting an excessively dark image.

   To even begin the process of adding split tones, you must first determine whether you want to use color or black & white.

   The appearance of a black-and-white photograph is altered when split toning is applied to it; it is no longer black and white. You can produce the appearance of blue and white, brown and tan, or any other color combination that you like.

   To achieve a sepia or cyanotype effect, you need to begin with a black-and-white photograph as your starting point.

   When applied to a color photograph, split toning enhances the colors that are already present in the image. Using the split toning options, you can select a more subdued tone. Additionally, you have the option of selecting tones that begin to make the other colors in the picture appear boring.

   If you want to correct the white balance, give it the appearance of a color film, or tint it without changing the colors, you should stick with working with a color picture.

   As soon as you are prepared to work with the treatment tool, select either a color or black and white picture from the available settings. On the main screen, it is located directly at the very top.

   You don't need to take any action if you select the color or have already made the transition to black and white.

2. Choose Your Highlight Color

Find the section in the Develop toolbar of Lightroom that is designated for split toning. For those of you who transformed your photo, it is now known as black and white. There is a choice between the HSL and the detail options.

If the screen is small, you should click the triangle immediately after the split toning process. A greater number of tools will be accessible in this scenario.

Decide the hue of your highlights to begin applying split tones. You have two distinct options to choose from when it comes to the tone that you want to apply to the highlights.

To get started, you will need to click on the gray box that is located next to the term Highlights. A pop-up window will follow. You can select a color from the rainbow that is displayed by using the mouse to make your selection.

If I wanted to create a glow that appeared more like one that occurs during the golden hour, I would go with orange. To give the impression that a black-and-white photograph is sepia, I would put dark tones on it.

You can select a different color by using the hue slider, or you may make minor adjustments to the color that you selected from the initial option.

Make the desired color selection by dragging the hue slider. Immediately, there will be a shift in the picture. With this, it is easy to observe how the color you select affects the overall appearance of the photo.

Additionally, you can simultaneously move the scale while holding down the **ALT** or **Option** key. Doing this will enable you to view the color in its full intensity. Having this information on hand could prove useful when working with softer color tones.

Finally, by adjusting the saturation slider, you can alter the amount of that color that is visible in the shadows during the editing process. If you move it to the left, the outcome will not be particularly significant.

Increasing the position of the slider to the right causes the color to become more prominent and stronger. As a result, the saturation level is increased.

3. Choose the Color of Your Shadows

The next step is to select the color shade that you intend to utilize. In addition, you have the option of altering the color of the shadows alone or the entire picture. You don't need to do both.

The procedures for this are identical to those that are used for the highlights. You are going to make use of the tools that are hidden in the shadows this time.

Simply clicking on the rectangle will bring up the color picker. It is also possible to use the sliders or a combination of the two.

When you have decided that you do not want to add any more color, you can return things to their original state by moving the saturation slider to the left edge of the screen. The highlights and the shadows can both benefit from the utilization of this.

4. **Balance the Highlight and Shadow Colors**

    You have not yet utilized the Balance tool, which happens to be the final split color tool. Using the balance slider, you can tell Lightroom how much of the photo consists of shadows and how much is concentrated in the brightness.

    You can make one of the colors you select for the highlights or shadows stand out more than the other by dragging this bar to the right.

    By default, the balance slider is positioned in the middle of the range. To add additional shadows or to make the colors of the shadows stand out more, you can move the slider to the left from where it is currently located.

    You can slide to the right to create additional shadows or to make the color of the shadows better stand out.

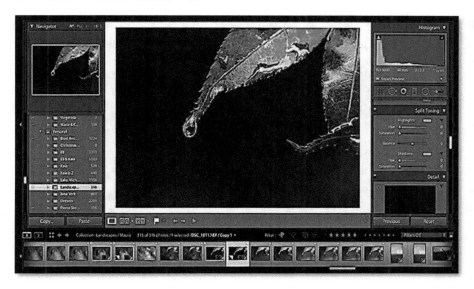

5. **Finish Your Edits in Lightroom**

    Lightroom does not alter the files in any way because it is an editor. You have the option of returning to those split toning settings if you change your mind about the colors being too intense.

Playing around with split tones is not only enjoyable but also simple because of this, in addition to the fact that the result can be seen immediately.

If you experiment with a few different color combinations, you could find one that you like. You can also experiment with the sliders to see what results you get.

After you are finished with split toning, you can utilize the other tools that Lightroom provides to make the picture look even more impressive. The HSL panel alters each color on its own, as opposed to merely modifying the highlights and shadows of the image. This can also assist you in editing hues with inventive methods.

When working with an image that has a split-tone effect, you need also to adjust the white balance, exposure, curves, and the slider that controls the shadows and highlights.

By using split toning, you can experiment with the colors present in a photograph. Having said that, split toning is another method that may be utilized to address troubles. By applying split toning to color photographs, it is possible to correct the colors or create creative effects that give the impression that the photographs were taken from a movie.

The blacks and whites of a black-and-white photograph are transformed into a distinct color through the process of split toning. There is a lot of interest in using this for sepia coloring.

If you don't know how to use the split toning section in Lightroom, it could be quite detrimental to the quality of your photographs. This is true regardless of how you utilize Lightroom.

Through the use of the straightforward sliders and/or color picker that are included in your Lightroom split tone tool, you can make the colors in any photograph appear as they should.

CHAPTER 11

USING PEOPLE VIEW

People View

The User Interface of Lightroom Classic is conventional. A new slider has been added to the revamped **'People View'** area of Lightroom's user interface.

Activating 'People View' in Lightroom

Located in the top left corner of your screen is the Lightroom icon. Launch Lightroom and click on it. Navigate to the Preferences menu by clicking on Tools. Launch the Preferences window and select Lightroom from the left-hand list to begin using it. Find the **Advanced** option in the right-hand column and click on it. Verify that the **Feature Photo** is selected as the default **People View** in the **People View** section.

How to Adjust the People View Effect in Lightroom

You can tweak the appearance of people's features slightly in the People's view. Typically, three modifications are made:

- A new editing window will pop up when you press **Ctrl+M**. Make use of the window's selection tool. To switch between People View and Background, simply click on an image in the drop-down menu and move it to the desired location. Before you return to Lightroom Classic to complete your selection, close the window.

- In Lightroom Classic, access the Look menu by pressing **Ctrl+Shift+L**. The items you selected will be displayed on the menu when you see them. Locate the magnifying glass in the lower left corner; choose tools that can be accessed by selecting **Refine Selection**. It will help you see your choice more clearly in the People's view. Using the zoom tool, you may rotate the pick. If you want something badly enough, you can change your behavior to get it. Switch back to Lightroom CC when you exit Lightroom Classic.

- Lightroom Classic now has a new Edit window that may be accessed by hitting a sequence of keys. You can restore the previous state of the people view and remove the item you selected from this window. Click the **Save & Quit** button at the upper right to exit edit mode.

Quick Develop and Auto Tone

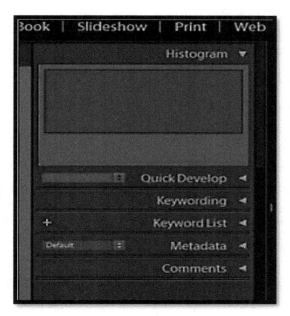

Lightroom is tailored to a specific type of photographer, yet there have been requests for a **Quick Develop** mode and an **Auto Tone** function. For those who are having problems navigating Lightroom CC, this will show you where the Quick Develop and Auto Tone sliders are located. A common question is whether there is a similar option in Lightroom Classic CC for activating the Auto Tone feature. The answer is yes. To toggle the auto tone in Lightroom CC on or off, just right-click on it and select **On/Off.**

How to Activate the Quick Develop Button

The Develop Module's Quick Develop button is on the sidebar.

- Right-click the Develop Module and choose **Edit**. That's all it takes to activate the **Quick Develop** button in Lightroom Classic.

- To activate the module in the Connections group, locate it in the Edit panel and look for the **Enable/Disable Developer Panel** option; next, click the radio button in the top right corner of the box.

- Locate the **Quick Develop** option on the Develop Module's Group page and toggle it on.

How to Enable the Auto Tone Key in Lightroom

Navigating to the Group page from the Project page in the Develop Module will lead you to this key.

- To activate Auto Tone in Lightroom, locate and press the **Auto Tone** button.

- It's as simple as clicking the **Auto Tone** button once you locate it.

- Click the **Auto Tone** button on the Develop Module's Group page.

Guidelines for Using Lightroom Classic's Auto Tone and Quick Develop

An excellent feature of Lightroom is the ease with which colors can be changed. You need to be strategic while using this tool if you want the color changes to stick. If you're familiar with Lightroom, you might recognize these features as Quick Develop and Auto Tone. Whatever you call them, they both describe ways to make your images pop.

1. **Quick Develop**

   From the Photo menu, choose Quick Develop to start the process. After that, decide the color space you wish to employ.

2. **Auto Tone**

   Next, select Auto Tone from the Photo menu, and last, click the Auto Tone tab.

3. **Speed Dial**

   Select your first image and then activate the Speed Dial function.

4. **Bevel/Grind Tool**

   The Bevel/Grind Tool option is located on the screen's right side.

5. **Focus Mask**

   Once you've chosen your subject, go to the right side of the screen and press the **Focus Mask** button.

6. **Darken**

   Press the **Darken** button that you'll see on the left.

7. **Luminosity Mask**

   Find and select the **Luminosity Mask** button in the top right corner.

8. **Hue/Saturation Mask**

   Select the **Hue/Saturation Mask** option on the right-hand side.

9. **Vibrance**

   In the upper right corner, click on the **Vibrance** button.

10. **Power**

    On the right side, press the **Power** button.

Merging Photos with HDR Panorama

If you've ever attempted to create an HDR photo using Lightroom and Photoshop, you know how challenging it can be. For HDR photos, post-processing is a common way to make them look more authentic. Automatic is the default setting in Lightroom. This provides you with three photos: one where you can adjust the shadows alone, one where you can adjust the highlights alone, and one where you can leave everything as is.

Things are not looking good at the moment. If you want to shoot an HDR image quickly, you can use these two applications together. Make use of the fantastic HDR picture Photo Merge tool if you like to create a stunning full-color image with enhanced clarity.

Merging HDR Panorama Photos in Lightroom is a breeze when you follow these steps:

- To start, navigate to the **Lightroom web interface**. After launching, go to **Lightroom's File menu** and select **Site Preferences**. Go to the bottom right and click on **Advanced**. When the pop-up window appears, click the **Merge Photos** box located on the left side. Press the **Save** button to commit your changes.

- Then, launch the Lightroom app on your mobile device. Select the **camera icon** located in the upper left corner. Once you've decided on an image in **Capture One**, you may use Keyframe to capture it. Choose the picture with an HDR image adjacent to the default picture in the list.

- Hold on a second. You can finish by clicking in the lower right corner of the screen. An emerald cloud is required. Pressing the cloud button will display the updated image.

- For the **Merge and Retouch** option, choose it. On the right side, you should see two buttons. Merge and Retouch are the names of these tools.

Merge and Retouch

Selecting the merged image is instantaneous upon clicking the **Merge and Retouch** button. Just below the join button, you'll see a Retouch button. Select the Retouch option. To create a smooth HDR panorama, it is necessary to merge the shots and adjust the highlights and shadows separately.

Just drag the little arrow to the right to reposition the shadows and highlights. If you want optimal results, test things out on both ends. You can merge all your HDR panorama images with a single click of the Unite button.

Installing Presets

Lightroom CC (32-bit) and Classic (64-bit) take a long time to set up, which is a problem with the preset system. After that, find the plus sign (+) in Lightroom's upper right corner and click it to rapidly add your profiles to the custom presets tab. Once you've added the Lightroom presets, you can customize their appearance to enhance your images.

The camera may utilize different settings when rendering the JPG file instead of the RAW file when you change the file type from original to JPG and save the files in the Camera Roll. You should convert your RAW files to JPGs before applying a preset. In this approach, your original images can be used within that preset.

Configuring Presets in Lightroom Classic (64-bit) and Lightroom CC (32-bit) Personalized Settings:

- Use the sliders to crop, blend, clone, change the roundness, tilt, and work with stacked negatives to change the picture.
- You can easily make changes and edits by cloning a section of your image and repositioning it. You have to recreate your previous successes for this strategy to be effective.
- Adjust the brightness of various areas of the shot using the buttons, and make sure it's uniform across the frame. Next, adjust the contrast settings as needed.

Presets in Lightroom

Here are a few examples:

- The Element, Da Vinci Resolve, Levels, Contrast, and Tonal Contrast are among them. You will apply these presets to your raw files.

- Lightness can be adjusted by dragging the main and secondary buttons. In situations where the topic is either too dark or too illuminated by a window, this comes in handy.

- When editing videos, it's common practice to utilize a cartoonish background to bring the subject into focus. To maintain their focus on the most intriguing section of the frame, this is often altered. This is a fantastic method for consistently achieving softer Bokeh while shooting animals. The person's eyebrows will also be affected, in most cases.

Post-Processing Tips: Using Presets and Rounded Edges

Lightroom presets are customizable, which makes them JPEG files incompatible. Raw files are compatible with Lightroom's presets. To make your images look better, this post will show you how to utilize Lightroom presets to make them sharper and how to trim the edges. In the layer you're currently working in, press and hold the word icon that appears next to the adjustment icon on the right side. Then, drag the circle clip to the desired location.

Leave it alone and let Lightroom do the rest. Because of the changes, no other layers in the stack will be affected. Also, give those levels the Lightroom custom effects you made. Press and hold the **angle** symbol while dragging the corresponding arrow to the right. After that, complete the task at hand. Here, I employed the Level scale. Rather than using the Linear Bias slider, consider using the N (Neutral) slider for a flatter appearance.

Keep in mind the proper technique for using the **Right-Hand Tool** at all times. Always make sure the sliders you choose are appropriate for the adjustments you intend to make. In general, you can adjust the sharpness of your photo using the angle slider. Just drag the button adjacent to the click icon to the right, and then drag the click icon to the right again, to modify the numbers.

Hold down the **sign icon** and drag the **cloud icon** in the center to the right to highlight the rounding feature. Just like before, turn on the shake feature. Because of how unpleasant the smooth edges are, most individuals would prefer not to wear it.

Enhancing Highlight Correction on JPEG Images

Lightroom includes an adjustment layer named Highlight Corrector that you may utilize to enhance the brightness or clarity of your JPEG images. If the remainder of your image is blurry, this could be useful. Before adding the Highlight Corrector Adjustment Layer to the photo layer, choose Highlights from the menu. By adjusting the Highlight Color slider and clicking the Highlights button, you may modify the quantity of the Highlight Corrector Adjustment Layer.

Place your images on the map.

You can easily layer photographs and set objects on the map with this module. You may pan the map and select which layers to show or hide. Simply click on an item to select it. Use the Resize option down below to check if everything fits snugly. Before continuing, ensure that the Map module is added if it isn't already.

Installing Lightroom Map Module

1. In Lightroom CC, select your Camera Profile and then hit the **Import New Folder** option up there. The module will be enhanced by this.

2. When you click **OK**, Lightroom will automatically add the .zip file to your library. The map module on your camera will then be able to function. Because adding map features to a consumer DSLR is much more of a pain, a

professional DSLR might be the way to go if you're in the market for one. To expedite the procedure, save the file as MAP.plist.

3.   First, save the file. Then, under Lightroom's settings, select **Map Pro**. Set the size of the square to 2048 x 2048. Click **OK** to commit the modifications.

Lightroom Tip: Enhancing the Map Pro with Distance Markers

To take advantage of the Map Pro Module in Lightroom, there are a few things you must do after obtaining it. The Map Pro Map file can be found in the **File** > **New Map** module. Set the map's dimensions to 4096 x 4096.

- Use **File** > **Open** to access the file. Simply display the name of the GPS device instead of the standard map center.

- Return to the Map module by selecting **File** > **Open**.

- To add an item to the map, just press the button and then choose the desired location. Not picking a random area on the map can prevent the GPS from accurately determining the beginning and end of your object. Instead, be specific. To accomplish this, select Convert to a coordinate map from the menu. Push the OK button to commit the modifications.

CHAPTER 12

CREATIVE TOOLS AND ADVANCED PHOTO MANAGEMENT

Lightroom is fantastic at preventing duplicate photographs from ending up in your folders. More than one collection can have a reference to the same image, and any modifications made to a file in one collection will reflect in all the other collections instantly.

Do you wish you could experiment with the file's appearance without modifying the original? Another feature that is helpful right now is the virtual copy.

1. Press the letter G while holding down the image selection toggles to the Grid view.

2. It is simple to create a new collection named Virtual Copies. To add an item to the Collections panel, simply click the **addition sign (+)** symbol that appears to the right of the title. Be careful to incorporate the selected image.

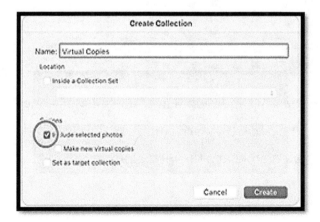

NOTE: To create a virtual copy, press **Command+'** (apostrophe) or **Ctrl+'** on your keyboard.

3. Use the context menu that appears when you right-click the image to select **Create Virtual Copy.**

4. To make it three items, add one more virtual copy.

These newly created files are virtual copies of the initial picture. Each version can be edited in the Develop module; when you do, the modified versions will appear as separate images.

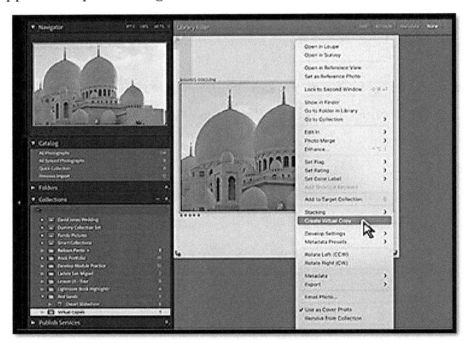

Despite their seeming independence, there is just one physical copy of the picture. This is because they are complete duplicates that are not associated with the original. Well, that's the virtual part.

To test various editing choices, you can make several virtual copies of a photo without significantly increasing the amount of space on your hard disk. You can compare the two virtual copies side by side to see which one you prefer.

5.   By selecting all three images and pressing the **N** key on your computer, you will get a comparison of your changes. To go back to the Grid view, press the **G** key.

An excellent feature in Lightroom Classic is the virtual copy's function, which allows you to edit or modify an image without copying the file. Follow these steps to create virtual copies:

1. **Startup Lightroom Classic:**

   To access the Library module, launch Lightroom Classic.

2. **Select Your Image:**

   In the Library module, locate the image you wish to create virtual copies of, and then click on it.

3. **Create Virtual Copy:**

   Several methods exist for creating a virtual copy:

   The right-click method:
   - Right-click on the picture you want to use.
   - Right-click on the image and select **Create Virtual Copy**.

   Keyboard Shortcut Method:
   - To use Windows, press **Ctrl + '**
   - For Mac: Press and hold **Cmd and '**

4. **Viewing Virtual Copies:**

   Both the original and virtual copies of the image will be displayed in the Filmstrip located at the Library module's base. You can find a little folded page icon in the lower left corner.

5. **Make Edits to Virtual Copies:**

   Click on it to select a virtual copy.

   To make any necessary changes, locate the Develop module. Neither the source picture nor any other copies will be affected by changes made to a virtual copy.

6.   **Compare Original and Virtual Copies:**

To quickly identify the variations between the original and virtual copies, select both and then utilize the **Before/After** view or hit the **backslash ** key.

7.   **Naming Virtual Copies:**

To distinguish between the various versions, you have the option to rename the virtual copies. To rename an existing virtual copy, just click and hold it, then choose **Rename**, and then enter the new name.

8.   **Delete Virtual Copies:**

If a virtual copy is no longer needed, you can delete it. The original or any additional copies will remain unaffected by this. When you right-click on the virtual copy, choose **Remove Photo** or hit the **Delete** key.

9.   **Exporting Virtual Copies:**

Now is the moment to save your modified virtual copies as separate files. You can accomplish this by using the Export dialog box after selecting them in the Library module.

Creating a virtual copy of an image allows you to experiment with various edits or versions without overwhelming your library with unnecessary duplicates. It's perfect for experimenting with various creative concepts or preserving many versions for various reasons.

Creating snapshots

When you take a snapshot, it records the exact moment in time when you made any edits to the image. Keeping a record in Snapshot form eliminates the need to visit the History panel to access an older version of your photo. Using snapshots, you can also recall various renditions of the identical image, such as a color and a black and white version.

Lightroom Classic's Develop module has a Snapshots panel that arranges Snapshots by letter.

Creating Snapshots in Lightroom Classic

There are three methods available in Lightroom Classic for creating a Snapshot. The first two are pre-set to operate with Lightroom Classic, while the third takes advantage of a feature known as Snapshot on Export.

1. Gain access to the Develop menu and choose New Snapshot by pressing Cmd-N (Mac) or Ctrl-N (PC).

   Depending on the current settings made in the Develop module, Lightroom creates a Snapshot. Just leave it as it is (the current date and time) or give it a name.

2. To create a snapshot using the settings that were applied to the image at a specific point in its development history, right-click on the **record** in the History panel and choose **Create Snapshot**.

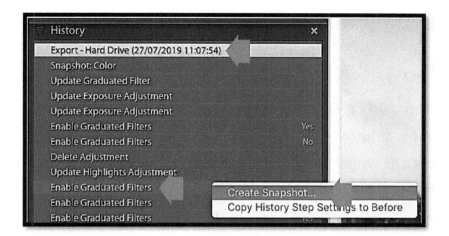

3. Whenever you export your photographs, the Snapshot on Export plugin will automatically take a snapshot. Each Snapshot is named using the export time and date. If you ever need to revert to an earlier version of an exported image, this feature will come in handy. Additionally, it will be helpful for anyone who sells their photographs.

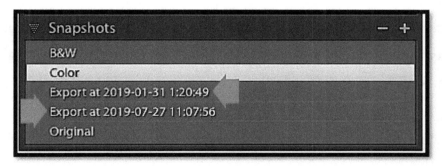

Using Snapshots in Lightroom Classic

You have these options for using Snapshots in Lightroom Classic.

1. **Record where you are in the Develop module**

    There is more than one method to navigate Lightroom's Develop module.

    Making two versions of the same image, one in color and one in black and white, is one example. One approach would be to take a snapshot after developing the color image.

203

After that, change the picture to black and white and take another picture when you're done. To switch between the two forms, click on the right Snapshots.

2. **Test Develop Presets**

Assume for the sake of argument that you are interested in giving Develop Presets a go with your first photo. It's conceivable that you're presented with multiple presets and aren't sure which ones you'll like.

Now you can choose the preset that suits you best by looking through them. When you discover a preset you like, use **Cmd-N** (Mac) or **Ctrl-N** (PC) to take a snapshot.

You'll have more than one Snapshot. To select your favorite option, you can now click on each one individually.

Tip: As a memory aid, rename your preferred Snapshot to Preset name [final] or something similar. Select **Rename** from the contextual menu that appears when you right-click on a Snapshot. You can delete a Snapshot by right-clicking on it and choosing Delete.

3. **Make comparisons**

You can easily tell which of the two Snapshots is your favorite.

o Click on the first picture with the right mouse button and select **Copy Snapshot Settings to Before**.

o To incorporate it into the image you are editing, choose the second Snapshot and click on it.

o Use the backslash (\) keyboard shortcut to switch between the previous and current choices to make the comparison.

Tip: The **Y|Y icon** on the toolbar allows you to toggle between the Before and After views. To access the Toolbar, use the T keyboard shortcut if it isn't visible.

4. **To replace Virtual Copies**

    Snapshots eliminate unnecessary Virtual Copies. A single copy of your image will be stored in the Catalog if you opt to use Snapshots instead. Finding lost Virtual Copies is unnecessary; a simple click on the stored Snapshots will reveal all the altered variations of your photo.

    TIP: Snap a shot and play about with the settings afterward. There will be no change to the image. But suppose you'd rather apply the edits to the Snapshot instead. Easy as pie. Simply right-click the **snapshot's name** to bring up a menu, and select **Update with Current Settings** to apply the latest changes.

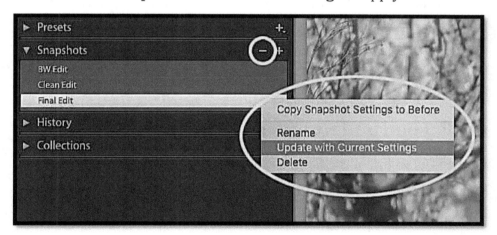

Snapshots vs. Virtual Copies

You can create several identical copies of an image using Virtual Copies. But there's a major catch: it's far too easy for identical virtual copies of an image to end up in many folders and collections.

Knowing the exact number of Virtual Copies a picture has is thus not possible in an instant. This makes it easy to lose track of all the picture edits you've made.

Snapshots are a great solution to this issue; under the Develop module, you can view a list of all the Snapshots associated with a particular photo. This is true even for digital copies of the picture.

Here's how it works.

For example, let's say you have 10 Snapshots labeled Snapshot_1, Snapshot_2, etc., and three Virtual Copies labeled Copy_1, Copy_2, and Copy_3.

Finding the total number of other Virtual Copies of Copy_1 is not a simple task. The most efficient method is to look for the picture in the Catalog panel's All Photographs Collection.

Conversely, you may view the total number of Snapshots in the Develop module's Snapshots panel.

What's more, whether you're working with the original file or a Virtual Copy, you can always view all of those Snapshots in the Develop module.

The one drawback of Snapshots is that, unlike Virtual Copies, they cannot be viewed in the Library module.

How to sharpen and use noise reduction

Located in the Detail panel is a Sharpening section that features four sliders. Radius, Detail, Amount, and Masking are the four of them. On top of those sliders, you can see the photo magnified to 100%. Press the tiny triangle on the panel's upper right to show or hide it. From this sample, it is impossible to discern the level of sharpening.

1. Click the larger image in the center of the sample area once to obtain a full-size view. Simply reposition the image to better observe the sharpening effect. When deciding how much to sharpen, this will be useful.

2. The Amount slider lets you adjust the amount of sharpening applied to the image; it's that easy. While dragging, hold down the **Option** or **Alt** key to

display a black-and-white sample. You can observe the sharpness more clearly with this.

You can adjust the amount of blurring around the pixel's periphery by dragging the Radius scale. You can't see this by simply adjusting the Radius option, so here's a method.

3.   Move the slider by pressing and holding the Alt or Option key. The image becomes grayscale when you shift it to the left. To get a better look at the edges, tilt it to the right. The details that are visible at the edges are the ones that are sharpened. In terms of potential enhancements, there is no gray area.

Proceed to the Detail slider after you have adjusted the Radius. More texture or detail will be brought to light in an image when you drag the Detail slider to the right. However, if you tilt it too far to the right or left, it will begin to make a sound. That should be noted.

4.   You can adjust the Detail slider to any number you like while holding down the Option or Alt key.

To restrict the sharpening method, use the Masking option. To sharpen only the edges, this creates a black-and-white mask. Sharpening will be applied to the white areas, but not to the black ones.

5.   By dragging the Masking slider to the right while holding down the Option or Alt key, you can adjust the area that will be sharpened. Holding down the Option/Alt key will make the image considerably easier to see. It won't make a screeching sound when you sharpen everything uniformly.

Press the **power button** in the top left corner of the Detail panel to get a **before** and **after** image of your sharpening. Press it once again to restore its sharpness. Now you can verify if you've added the correct amount.

Noise can be addressed when sharpening is complete. Pictures can have noise in them if either the shutter speed was too fast (due to the low light) or the image was overly sharpened.

The Noise Reduction section allows you to eliminate two distinct types of noise. The first is luminance noise, the primary cause of visual blurring. As the Luminance slider is shifted to the right, the cacophony begins to fade. By adjusting this slider, you can muffle 90% of the unwanted sound.

To restore lost detail after adjusting the Luminance slider, just drag the **Detail slider** to the right. Once you've made these changes, simply move the tool to the right slightly to re-add depth. The benefits of luminance noise reduction are diminished as the Detail and Contrast levels are increased, mostly because they tend to cancel each other out. Keep it in mind.

6. If you want a good-looking picture, set the Luminance Noise Reduction slider to 50, the Detail slider to 50, and the Contrast slider to 0. Just toggle the power switch in the Detail panel to see how your changes look, and then click it again to turn it back on.

Depending on whether the noise appears as red, green, or blue dots, you can adjust one of three settings. Shadows are the most common places for this to appear, and it happens frequently with some cameras. Shift the Color slider to the right until the dots no longer have any color to eliminate that type of noise. Finally, restore some of the lost detail and smooth it out to make it look balanced.

If you sharpen an image too much, removing the noise will make it smoother again. You should also do this if the file is high in ISO. Images are sharpened to a greater extent when additional noise is introduced to them, particularly when the Detail option is used. Therefore, it is recommended to add a small amount of noise reduction whenever you apply heavy sharpening in the Detail box.

The Detail panel's lower half is devoted to noise reduction. Contrast this with acoustic flooring. Noise, in the context of digital photography, refers to the random electrical signals picked up by the camera's sensor, which can distort the image. In low-light conditions, these spurious signals stand out more clearly because the sensor receives less accurate readings. This is why improperly exposed images often have noise issues.

For minor noise issues, you can use Lightroom Classic's basic noise-reduction options. You may adjust the amount of brightness noise and color noise separately using the sliders. Once you grasp the distinction between the two, solving the problem is as simple as adjusting the matching set of buttons to the correct value. My method for distinguishing between color noise and brightness noise is as follows:

- Luminance noise closely resembles the grain seen in films. Like in other blue-sky regions, the brightness varies while the color remains rather constant.
- Specks with multiple colors, such as Christmas tree lights, can be identified as color noise. The shadows are a common place to find these objects.

Blue skies are more likely to cause headaches when luminance noise is present. Before and after the repair, the image below (at a 3:1 zoom) shows a blue sky with the typical fuzzy indicators of luminance noise. I smoothed out the sky tones by adjusting the Luminance slider.

Note: Keep in mind that you can avoid using noise reduction altogether by adjusting the Masking slider up top if you'd rather not sharpen the noise. A greater number for Detail helps retain minute details, and a higher value for Contrast sets the degree of edge recognition utilized to locate noise; both sliders can be used to fine-tune the results.

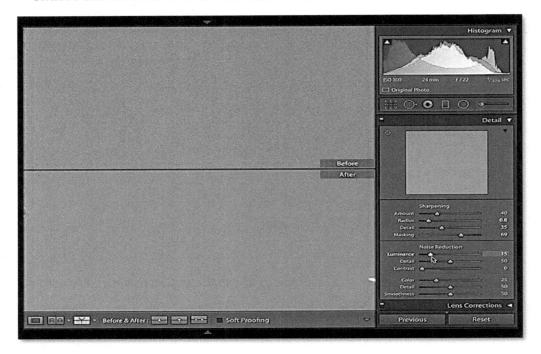

Below is an image comparing the **Before** and **After** appearance of an ISO 800 photo, shot at a 3:1 zoom. Color=25 is a good default setting for most images taken at lower ISO levels. To remove as many of the haphazard multicolored dots as possible, keep dragging the Color slider upwards if you can still detect color noise. Its operation can be fine-tuned by using the Detail (similar to brightness) and Smoothness (which aids in eliminating color mottling artifacts at higher ISOs) sliders.

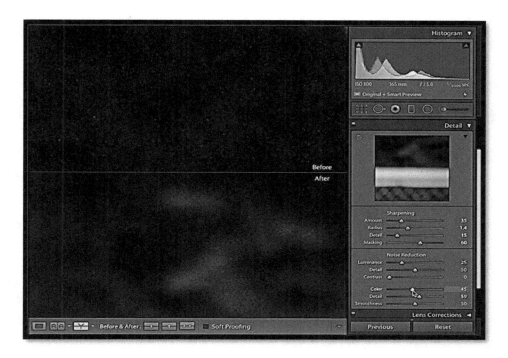

Remember that details will be lost when using any form of noise reduction; your image can end up looking like a watercolor painting if you drastically lower the noise level. Having a little noise with more information is usually preferable to having mostly empty pixels with little noise.

If you want your photos to stand out more in Adobe Lightroom Classic, you should use the sharpening and noise reduction tools. Here is the lowdown on how to use and enhance Lightroom Classic's noise reduction features:

Sharpening:

1. **Import Your Photo:**

   Bring the picture you want to work on into Lightroom Classic.

2. **Go to the Develop Module:**

   To begin, locate the **Develop** button in the top right corner.

3. **Navigate to the Detail Panel:**

On the screen's right side, you should see the **Detail** panel.

4. **Zoom In:**

To have a clearer view of the features you'll be working with, click on the image. To do this, use the Navigator panel located in the top left corner.

5. **Adjust Amount:**

To modify the level of sharpening, adjust the **Amount** slider located in the **Sharpening** section of the Detail panel. Sharpening too much could lead to imperfections, so proceed with caution.

6. **Adjust Radius:**

To modify the size of the enhanced features, move the **Radius** slider. More significant details are covered by greater values, whereas smaller values pay more attention to little details.

7. **Adjust Detail:**

Adjusting the **Detail** slider impacts the level of sharpening applied to high-frequency data. A lower value emphasizes bigger details, while a higher one emphasizes finer ones.

8. **Adjust Masking:**

You can prevent smooth color sections from becoming stronger by repositioning the **Masking** slider. While dragging the scale, keep the Alt (Option) key pressed to reveal the mask, to prevent the sharpening of smooth areas, such as the sky, mask more.

Noise Reduction:

1. **Navigate to the Detail Panel:**

   Remain in the **Detail** panel.

2. **Adjust Luminance Noise Reduction:**

   Lower the noise in your photo's overall luminance by dragging the **Luminance** slider in the **Noise Reduction** area. Be careful not to remove too much data.

3. **Adjust Detail and Contrast:**

   To get the optimal balance between eliminating noise and preserving features, adjust the **Detail** slider. Using the **Contrast** slider, you can adjust the level of contrast in areas where noise reduction has been applied.

4. **Adjust Color Noise Reduction:**

   Underneath the **Luminance** column, you should see the **Color** slider. You can adjust it so that your image is free of color noise.

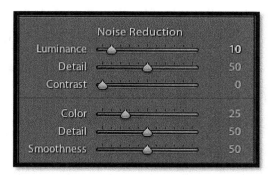

5. **Fine-Tune with Detail and Smoothness:**

   Shift the **Detail** and **Smoothness** sliders to improve the color noise reduction. The Smoothness value aids in the elimination of artifacts, while the information value increases the retention of color information.

6. **Preview Changes:**

By checking the **Preview** box located at the top of the Detail panel, you can observe the difference between the appearance of your adjustments to sharpness and noise reduction before and after they were made.

7. **Export or Continue Editing:**

By the time you are satisfied with your photo, you have the option to either export it or continue modifying it in the Develop module.

Keep in mind that you want to improve the photo's appearance without introducing any undesirable effects, so you should experiment with different levels of sharpening and noise reduction to find the sweet spot. While keeping an eye on the picture's quality and features, play around with these sliders.

Using presets to speed up your workflow

The use of presets, or themes, allows you to give your images a broad variety of styles and looks. Presets are a terrific way to save time when editing. With these, you can easily edit numerous images at once with the click of a mouse.

Do this to use settings that will make your work faster:

- First things first, launch **Adobe Lightroom Classic** and add the images you wish to edit to the library.

- To access the **Develop** module, either select the **Develop** tab in the top right corner of the screen or press the **D** key on your keyboard.

- The **Presets** panel can be found on the left side of the window in the Develop module. The + sign in the left panel will take you to a menu where you can choose **Presets**. If it isn't visible, you can make it so.

- Lightroom comes with a few pre-installed themes, but if you want even more customization options, you can always download more or create your own. By selecting the folder containing the presets, you may view their contents. To observe how a preset alters the selected picture, simply click on it.

- Simply clicking on the name of the preset will apply it. Immediately after applying the preset settings, you will be able to observe the effects on your photo.

- You may have to make a couple more adjustments to the presets before they match your photo, but they are a good starting point. In the **Develop** section, you'll find sliders that let you adjust various parameters, such as exposure, contrast, and color balance.

- You can adjust your settings if you notice that you occasionally make modifications that are extremely similar to one another. Hit the + button in the **Presets** panel, then choose **Create Preset**. Give your preset a name, and last, choose whatever parameters you wish to include in it.

- You can speed up the process by applying presets to multiple photographs simultaneously. In either the Library or the Filmstrip sections of the user interface, you can select the images that you wish to edit. After that, choose a preset to apply to those images.

- It's recommended to make individual changes to various factors before applying presets to many photographs. View the **Quick Develop** panel located on the right side of the screen once the preset has been added. Make any additional necessary modifications after that.

- Proceed to the **Library module**, select the desired photographs, and then hit the **Export button** once you have finished editing. Determine the correct options for the file's settings and the location to save it to.

Using the range mask feature to make selective adjustments

Using the Range Mask tool in Lightroom Classic, you can selectively edit the color or brightness of a specific area of your shot. With this powerful tool, you can enhance the appearance of your changes even further. To utilize the Range Mask function, follow these steps:

1. **Open Your Photo in the Develop Module:**

   Press the **Develop** module in Lightroom Classic after opening it.

2. **Make Initial Adjustments:**

   Before you apply the Range Mask, make any global modifications to your shot using the basic sliders in the Develop module.

3. **Choose an Adjustment Tool:**

   Select a tool for adjusting, such as the Graduated Filter, the Radial Filter, or the Adjustment Brush, from the available options.

4. **Apply the Adjustment:**

   Navigate to the area you wish to modify by dragging the adjustment tool. A few examples of such tools are the Adjustment Brush, the Radial Filter, which allows you to make circular alterations, and the Graduated Filter, which allows you to drag the filter across the sky.

5. **Open the Range Mask drop-down menu:**

   Scroll down until you find the **Range Mask** option once the modification has been made.

6.   **Choose Between Color and Luminance:**

You have the option to select Color and Luminance from the Range Mask menu.

o   **Color:** You can modify the appearance by selecting a certain color scheme.

o   **Luminance:** Adjustments can be made according to the brightness of the selected area.

Using Color Range Mask:

1.   **Select the Color Eyedropper:**

To select a color, click on the **eyedropper icon** that is located next to Color.

2.   **Click on the color you want:**

Select the color in the picture you want to include in the adjustment and click on it.

3.   **Adjust the Range Slider:**

For a more precise adjustment, you can use the **Amount** slider. This determines the color scheme utilized throughout the transformation.

4.   **Refine with Smoothness:**

The transition from the selected color to the other colors is made less obvious by adjusting the **Smoothness** slider.

Using Luminance Range Mask:

1.   **Pick out the Luminance option:**

With the Luminance Range Mask, select **Luminance** from the Range Mask dropdown menu.

2.   **Adjust Luminance Range:**

To adjust the brightness level range that the change will impact, press and hold the appropriate buttons. Adjusting the **Range** slider determines the brightness level range while adjusting the **Smoothness** slider makes the transition more subtle.

3. **Refine Your Adjustment:**

    To make the overall alteration more precise, use the sliders on the tool panel. You can achieve the desired effect by adjusting several settings, such as exposure, contrast, saturation, etc.

4. **Finish Editing:**

    After you're satisfied with the adjustments you've made, you have the option to either save the picture or make additional changes.

CHAPTER 13

WORKING WITH SMART PREVIEWS

Using Smart Previews

It can use smaller versions of the original picture called Smart Previews when:

- Working with photos in the Develop module (and Quick Develop panel) when the originals are offline, like when they're on a drive that's not plugged in?

- Syncing Lightroom Classic files to the cloud so that Lightroom on mobile devices can view them.

The Library module's previews (in Grid, Loope, Zoom, Survey, and Compare views) and the Smart Previews (stored in a separate file named Smart Preview.lrdata) are distinct.

Making Smart Previews

On Import

When you add new photos to Lightroom, make sure to make Smart Previews. Doing things this way is the best option. All you have to do is click the **Build Smart Previews** button on the right.

Images Already in the Catalog

After locating the images you wish to convert to Smart Previews from your library, choose them using the library drop-down menu.

In the **Previews** submenu, locate **Build Smart Previews** and select it.

Just below the bar, you'll see the **Original Photo** box; click on that to see a specific picture. A dialog window will then appear, asking whether you would like to create a Smart Preview:

The loading time of the teasers could be longer if you are working on multiple photographs simultaneously.

But once they're made, you can make changes, export, print, or edit them even if you don't have the originals.

Managing Smart Previews

Smart Previews are pretty much the only thing you need to do after setting them up.

You can still see how much space they are consuming and remove them if your laptop becomes too full.

Navigate to **Catalog Settings > File Handling** to check the storage use of your Smart Previews.

Then you'll be able to see how much storage space your Smart Preview file is hogging.

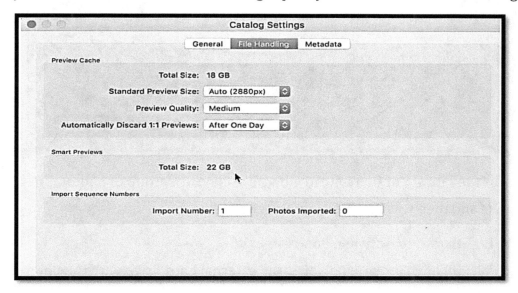

If you find that Smart Previews are taking up too much space, you can easily remove them by deleting them from images that you are no longer working with.

It is almost the same to do this with a single image as it is to create one.

The **Original + Smart Preview** option should be your button of choice. A box will then pop up asking if you would like to disable Smart Preview.

To access the Library option in Grid view, first choose a group of photos. There, click **Previews** and then **Get Rid of Smart Previews.**

Telling Lightroom to only use Smart Previews

Even if you still have the originals (i.e., the external hard drive with the photographs is still connected), you can instruct Lightroom to exclusively use Smart Previews.

To achieve this, go to Lightroom and look for the **Preferences** drop-down menu. Proceed to the **Performance** tab by clicking on it. There is a box for changing pictures. Check **Use Smart Previews** instead of **Originals**.

Use Smart Previews by going to **Lightroom > Preferences > Performance** Restarting Lightroom will be necessary thereafter.

Limitations of using Smart Previews

Be mindful of Lightroom's Smart Previews' limits while dealing with them, especially if you often use Photoshop or do HDR or panorama merges.

1. **Compatibility with Photoshop:** In terms of compatibility with Photoshop, neither the program nor any of its plugins will work with Smart Previews. You

must have access to the source files to use Photoshop to edit your images. Navigate to the Lightroom menu and choose Edit In > Photoshop to launch Photoshop and access the source image.

2. **HDR and Panorama Merges:** Merging photographs into High Dynamic Range (HDR) or panoramas is also not possible with Smart Previews. You must have access to the initial source files to complete these activities. Smart Previews might not be enough if your process requires a lot of work with HDR or panoramas.

3. **Quality and Adjustments:** When it comes to fine-grained modifications like noise reduction and sharpening, the 1:1 preview produced by a Smart Preview differs from the 1:1 view of the original RAW file. When compared to the original, high-resolution RAW files, the Smart Previews don't quite cut it. You should go back to the original file and tweak the noise reduction or sharpness settings if you made any changes; the Smart Preview might not be the best place to see how they turned out.

If you prefer to edit in Lightroom and rarely use Photoshop or make HDR merges, Smart Previews can help you organize your workflow and edit more efficiently. To guarantee the highest quality and accuracy in your adjustments, you may need to depend more on the original files if your work involves these sophisticated procedures.

CHAPTER 14

DESIGNING PHOTO BOOKS AND PRESENTATIONS

Whether you're looking to preserve memories from a vacation, showcase your work, or commemorate a significant occasion with loved ones, a picture book is a classy and elegant way to do it. You may find everything you need to create fashionable books in the Book module. You have the option to either export them to PDF and print them on your printer, or you can directly upload them to Blurb for printing.

How To Use The Book Module To Create Photo Books

Setting up a photo book

You may not be able to view the photographs that are already placed in the page layouts in the workspace if you haven't explored the tools and controls of the Book module yet. Get everyone on the same page by clearing the floor and arranging their desk before you begin.

1. Locate the **Clear Book** button on the top taskbar and click on it. The header bar can be accessed by selecting **View > Show Header Bar**.

2. In the Book Settings panel, located at the top of the right panel group, choose **Blurb Photo Book** from the Book menu. Then, in the Size drop-down menu, choose **Standard Landscapes**. On the Cover, choose Hardcover Image Wrap. For the Paper Type, choose Standard. And for the Logo Page, choose On. The current printing cost for the book is displayed at the bottom of the panel.

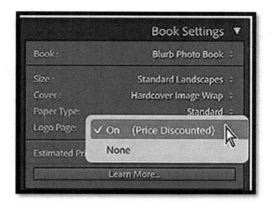

3. To switch to a multi-page view, if it isn't already selected, use the button on the far left of the toolbar at the bottom of the desk. Under View, you can disable the Show Info Overlay feature.

4. You can view the options by going to **Book > Book Preferences**. You can choose to crop the images to fit the image cells or zoom in and make them bigger. You have control over how text behaves and can disable Autofill for new books. After making your selections, close the Book Preferences window.

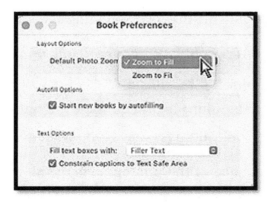

The Autofill feature is enabled by default. The collection's images would already be in the typical book arrangement if you had just launched the Book module. Automatically generated layouts are a good starting point when you aren't sure what you want for your new book.

5.   The Auto Layout panel can be enlarged as needed. After going to the **Auto Layout Preset** menu, choose the **One Photo Per Page** arrangement. Afterwards, hit the **Auto Layout** option. Move your cursor down the page to view all the images displayed in the workspace. To apply the **Left Blank, Right One Photo, With Photo Text** auto-layout setting, click the **Clear Layout** button once more.

6.   Take a look at the book's outcomes on the desk. To view all the page photos aligned on the two-page spreads in the Multi-Page view, scroll down if necessary. Pressing F7 or clicking the triangle on the left side of the screen will hide the left panel group, allowing you to make extra room. The images' size can be adjusted by moving the corresponding slider on the toolbar.

The process creates a book with a cover, individual pages for each image (numbered according to their appearance in the Filmstrip), and a special 38th page reserved for the Blurb logo. You have the option to conceal the Blurb badge page in the Book Settings panel if you want not to have a photo on it.

To adjust the sequence of the photographs in the reel before clicking Auto Layout, you must save your book.

Covers for Filmstrip books often feature the first image and back covers include the last image in the series. The Filmstrip counts the number of times each picture appears in the book. There were two instances of the first and last images—on pages 1 and 37—in addition to the cover.

Changing page layouts

Using an auto-layout setting will help you get your book written faster. Sections and pages can then be worked on separately to provide variation and depth to the design. But in this role, you will be required to create the blueprint for your book from the ground up.

1. Go to the **Auto Layout panel** and click the **Clear Layout** button.

2. Select **Solo Mode** from the context menu that appears when you right-click the Page panel header.

3. Double-click the **front cover** (the right side of the spread) in the Multi-Page view.

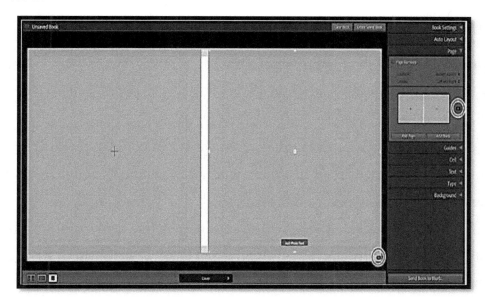

To view the front and back covers simultaneously, double-click the **thumbnail of the cover**; this will take you to a Single Page view. The yellow square in the middle indicates that the front cover photocell has been picked. You may see a visual representation of the standard cover layout in the Page panel. Along the spine of the book, there is a small text cell and two picture cells, the middle of which is indicated with crosshairs.

4.   To change the page layout, see the Page panel for a thumbnail of a sample layout or look in the lower right corner of the workspace for the cover spread, and then click the **black button with a gray triangle** that says **Change Page Layout**.

5.   You can view all the available cover layout designs in the page template picker by scrolling down. Squares filled with horizontal lines denote text cells, whereas gray regions with crosshairs in the center indicate image cells. Select the third template from the drop-down option. There are three text cells in this template: one on the spine, one on the front cover, and one on the back cover. You can see this by looking at the single crosshair in the middle of the spread. The image cell spans the two covers.

Adding text and captions to your photo book

The Book module has multiple methods for adding text to pages, and each one has its own set of benefits:

- The text cells that are included with the page layout templates cannot be removed, moved, or resized. Changing the cell padding, though, allows you to reposition text wherever on the page.

- The layout includes an image description, which is a text cell linked to one picture. It can be repositioned to appear higher or lower on the page, and it can even go above or below an image.

- A page caption, as opposed to a picture caption, is a text cell that scans the entire page. The entire width of the page is occupied by the page titles. You can reposition the text on the page by dragging and dropping the cells and then adjusting the cell padding. Anywhere in your layout you choose, you may add custom text with this.

Even if the website's layout template doesn't include any fixed text cells, you can still write captions for each picture on the page. With the ability to establish fixed text cells and photo captions, you can display text, titles, or captions that are automatically retrieved from your photos' information.

The state-of-the-art text tools in the Book module's Text styling allow you to style the text in anyway you choose. With the Text Adjustment tool, you may visibly alter type attributes or use sliders and numbers to make changes.

Working with text cells

Pages with text cells that are part of a template stay where they are. Instead, you can change the cell space to move the text exactly where you want it on the page. The space around the text in a cell is called cell padding.

1. To see how your whole book is laid out, click the **Multi-Page View** button. To see it better, double-click just below the cover picture. Click in the middle of the front cover to pick the fixed text cell.

    TIP: To choose a page or spread instead of the layout's text and picture cells, click near the thumbnail's edge or just below it.

2. Make the Type panel bigger. To use text that you enter instead of picture information, make sure the Text Style Preset is set to Custom.

3. You can choose a font and type style from the choices below the pre-set setting. American Typewriter in Bold is a good pick. When you click on the Character color swatch, the color choice will appear. Click the **black dot** at the top of the picker and then press **Return** or **Enter** to close it. Leave the opacity at 100 and

make the text size 47 points. Click the **Align Center** button in the bottom left corner of the Type box.

4. Type any word you like, press **Return** or **Enter**, and then type another word you like. Double-click the most recent word to select it. To make the text bigger, type **90 pt** in the Size text box.

5. To open the type attribute options, move your mouse over the text and click on the **white triangle** to the right of the Character color swatch. Bring down the leading to 73.8 points. Leading is how far away the text you've chosen is from the line above it. In the bottom panel, find the Align Right button and click it; this will align both lines of text to the right. The words will stand out more this way.

    TIP: Once you change the Leading number, the Auto Leading button will show up below the text adjustment controls. This makes it simple to get back to the original setting. The Auto Kerning button does the same thing.

6. If you click inside the text box but not on the text, the cell stays picked but the text is not. Then, open up the Cell screen. First, **click the box next to Link All** and remove it; this will make the top space 60 pixels wide.

Working with captions

You can move page and picture caption cells up and down, but you can't move text cells that are built into layout styles. You need to change the padding to move labels across the page. One-page description text cells and picture caption cells can be added to each page, even if the page template doesn't have any text cells.

1.   If you right-click the title of the Type panel, you can turn off Solo Mode. Then open the Type panel and make the Text panel bigger.

     TIP: You don't have to use the floating buttons on the page to add a picture or text description. The choice can be made in the Text panel instead.

2.   Move the mouse to page 1. There is no set text cell in this page's template, so there is no underlining. First, click on the picture. Then, click on the **Add Photo Text** button. The Photo Text settings will appear in the Text panel. If you want to get rid of the picture description, press **Command+Z** or **Ctrl+Z.** Now, click the yellow line below the picture to switch from **Add Photo Text** to **Add Page Text**. When you click the **Add Page Text** button in the Text panel, the Page Text options show up.

     TIP: You can only use page captions for custom text. You can't set them to show picture details like photo captions can.

3.   There is a Top button in the Page Text controls. Click it. To put the page description at the top of the page, drag the Offset scale to 96 pt.

4.   Set up the Type panel, but use Regular instead of Bold. Size should be set to 30 points, and Tracking should be set to 3 points. Click the Auto Leading button if it's on. Click the **Align Left button** and change the color to white. Then type what you want it to display. To break up the lines so the text fits the picture, press the **Enter** or **Return** key.

Fine-tuning type

The Type panel in Lightroom has powerful type tools that are also easy to use. These tools give you full control over how the text looks. You can change the features of a type in the Type panel by using the adjustment sliders and the number keys. The simple **Text Adjustment tool** lets you change the way your text looks in any view.

1. Check out the four settings below the Size and Opacity sliders in the Type panel. Now, delete any changes you've made.

   o **Tracking** changes how far apart the letters are in a group of text. There are two ways to change the way your text looks and how easy it is to read: make it look more open or bigger.

   o **Baseline** moves the chosen text around an imagined line called the baseline, which is what the text sits on.

   o **Leading** changes the amount of space between the text you've chosen and the line above it.

   o What **Kerning** does is change how far apart the letters are between some sets of two. Some pairs make the spacing between the letters look off because of the way they look together. You can fix this by moving the mouse between two letters.

2.   Pick out all the words in the front cover text box. The Text Adjustment tool is to the left of the Character color setting in the Type panel. To begin editing, click it.

3.   To change the text's size, drag across the pick horizontally. There is a small change in the different sizes of writing because of the change. To undo the change, press **Command+Z** or **Ctrl+Z**, or go to **Edit > Undo**.

4.   Drag the heading vertically over the selection to change it. To undo something, press **Command+Z** or **Ctrl+Z** or go to **Edit > Undo**.

5.   To turn off the **Text Adjustment tool** for now, press and hold the **Option** or **Alt** key. After that, choose the first word you wrote instead of the second one. Let go of the mouse button and the Alt or Option key. Then, hold down the **Command** or **Ctrl** key and drag horizontally over the text you want to erase. Watch it as you move the Tracking setting in the Type panel to −21 em.

6. Let go of the mouse button. Hold down the **Command** or **Ctrl** key and drag the mouse up and down over the text you want to move. Change the size to 6 points and click outside the word to get rid of it.

7. Press **F7** or go to **Window > Panels > Hide Left Module Panels** to make the words on the front cover bigger. You can move your mouse between the r and t in Portfolio by pressing the button keys. Make sure the tool for changing the text is still on. Drag the mouse to the right of the point where you want to put it. As you drag to set 61 em as the Kerning number, keep an eye on the Type field.

8. Pick out all the text and move the Leading tool until it looks good. The Text Adjustment tool is in the Type panel. Click it to turn it off. Click the **Multi-Page View** button in the Toolbar to see how your book is laid out as a whole. Double-click page 1 to go to the Single Page view.

How to use auto layout to automate your layout process

Choose a plan, and then click **Auto Layout** to have it done for you. To start over, click **Clear Layout.** Auto-layout can only be used for 240-page books when you send them to Blurb. You can have as many pages as you want when you export to PDF.

Customizing your background

The pages of a new book usually all have the same white background. You can change the color of the background, make the picture partly see-through, or choose a picture from a library. After that, you can design a page or the whole book.

First, you can add two more pages to your book.

1. Select **Add Page** from the menu that appears when you right-click on page 4. If you want to use the basic layout on page 5, right-click it and choose **Add Page**. When you right-click on page 6, a menu will appear. Choose **Add Blank Page** from that menu.

2. In the Multi-Page view, click on **page 6** to select it. Then, click the **Spread View** button in the Toolbar.

3. Expand the Background box. Remove the check mark from the box next to Apply Background Globally. Next, drag the picture to the Background panel's preview bar. Move the slider to 43 to make the picture less opaque.

4. Pick out the background color you want, then click on the color swatch next to it to bring up the color choice. It's about two-thirds of the way up the saturation scale on the right side of the color picker. To find a muted tone, drag the eyedropper cursor in the picker. Below, a color was chosen that has R, G, and B numbers of 98, 100, and 89, Press **Return or Enter** to close the picker.

5. In the Background panel, check the box next to Apply Background Globally. Then, in the Toolbar, click the **Multi-Page View** button.

   Your background is on all pages except the Blurb brand page, which only has the color. You can see it on pages 2, 4, 5, 6, and 7 and behind the pictures on page 2. On some pages, the background design is hidden by photocells.

6. Take the check mark off of the box next to the Background Color. Next, right-click on the picture in the viewing pane of the background. Select **Remove Photo**. Finally, turn off **Apply Background Globally.**

7. Pick page 2 in the Multi-Page view, and then turn on the **Background Color** setting again. Click on the color swatch to bring up the color choice. After that, click the black dot at the top of the choice. When you press Return or Enter, the color picker will stop.

Designing your book cover

People read your book's front cover as a two-page spread instead of two separate pages like the rest of the book. You can choose from several themes, though. First, click on the cover. Then, click on the small black button in the bottom right corner that has an arrow heading down. You'll see a pop-up menu with themes when you do this. It's used when you click on the one you want. You can put one picture on the front and one on the back of your first style. Last but not least, all of these examples have writing in them already. In the Text panel (see image below), which is on the right side of the Panels area, make sure that the Photo Text box is checked.

CHAPTER 15

IN-DEPTH EDITING WITH THE DEVELOP MODULE

You can change your pictures' color and tonal scale, crop them, get rid of red eye, and do other things in Lightroom Classic's Develop module. The source file stays the same no matter what changes you make in Lightroom Classic. When you use non-destructive editing, you don't change the source file. This is true whether the picture is straight from the camera or has been changed in some way, like a JPEG or TIFF. It saves the changes you make to a picture as a list of steps that can be used on the picture later. If you edit your picture without destroying it, you can try out different copies of it without losing any of the original data.

In the panels on the left side of the Develop module, you can pick pictures, see previews of them at different stages of editing, and use global presets. There is a place to work and look in the middle of the Develop area. You can do many things with the tools below the work area, like switch between **before** and **after** views and turn on **soft proofing**. The panels on the right give you tools and settings to change the way your pictures look.

A. Presets, Snapshots, History, and Collections panels **B.** Toolbar **C.** Histogram **D.** Photo Information **E.** Smart Preview Status **F.** Tool strip **G.** Adjustment panels

Understanding basic editing tools

You need to know how to use Adobe Lightroom Classic's basic editing tools to make your photos look better. If you want to learn how to use and understand some of the most basic editing tools, read this:

1. **Exposure:**

    What it does: It changes how bright your picture is in general.

    How to use: Find the **Exposure** slider in the **Basic** panel and use it. You can move it to the left or right to change the brightness of the picture.

2. **Contrast:**

    What it does: It changes how light or dark different parts of your picture are.

    How to use: You can learn how to use the **Contrast** tool in the Basic panel by moving it around. You can turn it up for more dramatic pictures or down for a softer look.

3. **Highlights and Shadows:**

    What it does: They let you change how bright your picture's highlights and shadows are.

    How to use: You can use it by moving the **Highlights** and **Shadows** buttons around. To bring out details in bright areas, turn down the highlights. To do the same in dark areas, turn up the shadows.

4. **White Balance:**

    What it does: It changes the color temperature of your picture in general.

How to use: To use, move the **Temp** slider in the Home panel to make the picture warmer (yellow) or cooler (blue). The **Tint** tool changes how much magenta and green are mixed.

5. **Clarity:**

What it does: This makes the middle tones more contrasty, which draws attention to small details.

How to use: If you want to learn how to use the **Clarity** tool in the Presence area, move it around. To make the texture pop out more, move it up. To make it look softer, move it down.

6. **Vibrance and Saturation:**

What it does: They let you change how bright the colors are in a picture.

How to use: To use, turn up **Vibrance** for a safer color boost that is more even. Turn up Saturation to make the color look better everywhere.

7. **Tone Curve:**

What it does: It lets you change the color range of your picture more precisely.
How to use: To change the highlights, midtones, and blacks separately, make an **S** curve in the Tone Curve box.

8. **HSL/Color Panel:**

What it does: This tool lets you change the hue, saturation, and brightness of every color.

How to use: In the HSL/Color box, find the tab for Hue, Saturation, or Luminance. Here's how to use it. The bars will change to match the color range you click on.

9. **Sharpening:**

What it does: It boosts the sharpness of your picture, which makes it better.

How to use: Adjust the Amount, Radius, and Detail sliders in the Detail panel to see how to use it. Masking lets you sharpen only certain areas.

How to adjust exposure, color, and tone

When you edit pictures in Adobe Lightroom Classic, you can change the exposure, color, and tone all of the time. This is a rough plan for how to make these changes:

Adjusting Exposure:

1. **Open Your Picture:**

   Now that you have your picture in Lightroom Classic, go to the **Develop module**.

2. **Basic Panel:**

   The Basic screen is on the right side of the screen. It's where the buttons for exposure are.

   You can change the brightness or darkness of the whole picture by moving the **Exposure** tool.

3. **Other Exposure Controls:**

   If you want to change the brightness of certain areas, use the **Highlights**, **Shadows**, **Whites**, and **Blacks** sliders.

Adjusting Color:

1. **White Balance:**

   For the right color temperature, change the White Balance setting in the Basic

   list. Click on a **neutral gray spot** with the eyedropper tool to get the right color.

2. **Vibrance and Saturation:**

   Make small changes to the Vibrance tool to bring out the best in soft colors without making them too intense.

With the Saturation tool, you can change how bright the colors are in general.

3. **HSL/Color Panel:**

In the HSL/Color box, you can change the specifics of each color.

Hue changes the color, Saturation changes how strong the color is, and Luminance changes how bright the color is.

Adjusting Tone:

1. **Tone Curve:**

Use the Tone Curve panel to make small changes to the highlights, shadows, and midtones.

If you change the RGB curve, you can change the general tone tweaks.

2. **Presence Panel:**

Click **Clarity** in the Basic panel to make the middle tones pop out more and Dehaze to get rid of any fog or haze.

3. **Detail Panel:**

Use the Sharpening and Noise Reduction sliders to change how sharp the picture is and get rid of noise.

Other Tips:

- **Graduated Filter and Radial Filter:**

With these tools, you can make certain changes. Different types of filters can be used to change the sky's color or draw attention to a certain place.

- **Presets:**

There are sets in Lightroom that can change your picture in a certain way. You can use them as a base and then improve them.

- **History Panel:**

  You can see what changes you've made in the History panel. If you don't like the change, you can go back to a state from before it happened.

  Please remember that these are just ideas. What choices work best for you will depend on the picture and how you want to use them. Move and use the different tools to make your picture look the way you want it to.

How to crop and straighten photos

In the Develop module, you can crop and straighten pictures using the tools and settings there. There is a crop line that you set in Lightroom Classic before you move and spin the picture around it. We can crop and fix things like this. You can also use the crop and level tools and move the picture around that way.

Lightroom Classic shows a grid of thirds inside the shape when you move or change the crop layer; this helps you arrange the picture's parts and helps you line up with the straight lines in a picture as you turn it.

Crop a photo

1. You can press **R** or pick the **Crop Overlay** tool from the list of tools. There is a line around the picture with adjustment bars that shows up.

2. To set the crop line, move the Crop Frame arrow into the picture or drag a crop handle. You can change the picture's width and height with the corner knobs.

    Note: To use the Crop Frame tool, drag a crop handle and then click on it.

3. The Hand tool lets you drag the picture inside the crop box to move it.

4. Choose **Constrain To Warp** if you want to keep the cropping box inside the picture area after the lens changes have been made. When you use Constrain To Warp, the shot will not be messed up.

5. Click the **Crop Overlay tool** or press **Enter** (Windows) or **Return** (Mac OS) to save the changes.

    Note: Press the **O** key to move between grid levels in the crop area. Make sure you only see the grid when you crop by going to **Tools > Tool Overlay > Auto Show**. To hide the grid, go to **Tools > Tool Overlay > Never Show.**

Crop to a specified aspect ratio

1. Pick out the Crop Overlay tool from the list of tools.
    There is a padlock button in the tool drawer that lets you change whether the crop settings are hard or soft.

2. The button next to the key that pops up says Aspect. Pick an aspect ratio from that list. Choose **Original** to set the photo's original size. In this case, if you want to use a different aspect ratio, press **Enter Custom**.
    Note: To get the Crop Overlay tool with the last ratio you used, press **Shift+A.**

    You can save five different crop ratios in Lightroom Classic. The old ones will be taken off the list if you make more than that.

3. To set the crop shape, you can use the **Crop Frame tool** or a crop handle.
    Note: If you hold down Shift while moving a crop handle, the aspect ratio will stay the same for now.

Switch crop orientation

1. Pick out the Crop Overlay tool from the list of tools.
2. Drag the picture into place to set the crop line.
3. Press the **X** key to go from landscape to portrait or portrait to landscape mode.

Straighten a photo

1. Pick the **Crop Overlay tool** from the toolbar and do one of these things:

- Use the Angle slider to turn the picture.
- Move the mouse away from a corner crop handle until the Rotate icon ↰shows up. This will turn the picture around. After that, drag the picture to turn it. The crop square is in the middle of the turn line.
- Select the **Angle tool** ⬤ and move the picture along the line you want to be at the top or bottom.

Note: If you choose the fix tool and press and hold Alt (Windows) or Option (Mac OS), a grid will show up to help you fix the picture.

Clear or undo a crop or straighten adjustment

1. In the toolbox for the Crop Overlay, click **Reset**.

Straightening and cropping an image

1. To get to the Loupe view from the **Develop** tab, press the **D** key.
   NOTE: In Lightroom Classic 2025, there is a tool called **Edit** to the left of the Crop tool. This lets you quickly leave a change and go back to the Basic panel, where you can make more changes.

2. The Crop Overlay tool▦ is in the circle at the top of the picture below. To get to it, click on it or press the letter **R**. In the group on the right, it's right below the Histogram. You can crop a picture and make it straight with the Crop Overlay tool.

3. A panel with options for each tool shows up at the bottom of the tool strip. Click on the circle on the left side of the picture above to use the Straighten tool. The pointer changes to a crosshairs pointer, and the level icon moves with you as you move across the sample picture.

4. This tool lets you draw a line that goes along the street in the background. When you let go of the mouse button, the picture turns so that your line is horizontal, and the Straighten tool returns to its place in the Crop Overlay tool choices. To go back and try again if you don't like the result, press **Command+Z** or **Ctrl+Z**. In the text box next to the Straighten tool slider, you can say what kind of turn you want. You can also drag the slider itself.

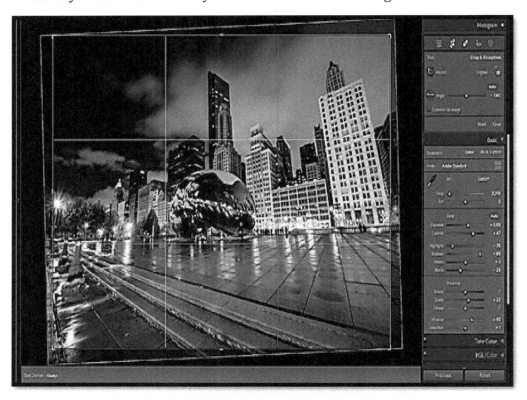

Lightroom puts a cropping box on top of the picture that has been straightened, and it moves it automatically to get the biggest crop that keeps the original aspect ratio. After that, the arched ends are cut off.

TIP: If you're cropping a picture by hand, make sure that the aspect ratio is locked and that the Original is chosen from the cutting Aspect menu. This will keep the image's basic size and shape.

The crop can be changed by moving any of the eight handles on the box. In the Tools > Crop Guide Overlay menu, you can pick from different grid outlines to help you crop by hand.

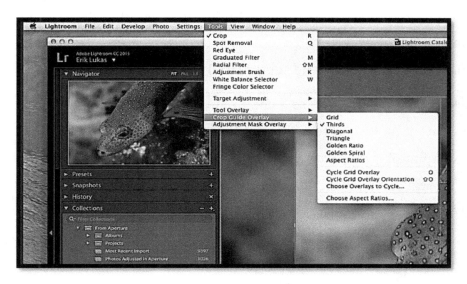

To hide the grid, go to **Tools > Tool Overlay > Never Show**.

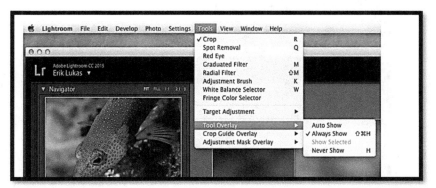

5. Press   **Return or Enter** to crop the picture, or click the **Crop Overlay** tool or the **Close button** in the bottom right corner of the tool group. You can always click the tool again to crop or turn it on and off.

Cropping to specific dimensions

Many times, photographers want to make sure that the crop of their picture stays the same as the ratio at which it was shot. In this case, for a DSLR frame, that ratio is 3:2. But sometimes you might want to change the ratio of your crop. For example, for Instagram you might want to make a square crop, for Facebook, you might want to make a bigger cover post, or wide shots (16:9).

Right-click on **Aspect** and choose a common photo size. This will appear as long as the Crop Overlay tool is chosen. Some of these are 1x1 (square size), 4x5 (great for making 8x10 photos), and 16x9. In this case, choose the 16x9 crop to make the picture look a bit more like a movie. It doesn't take long for the crop overlay to change sizes, and the 16x9 crop now caps its size.

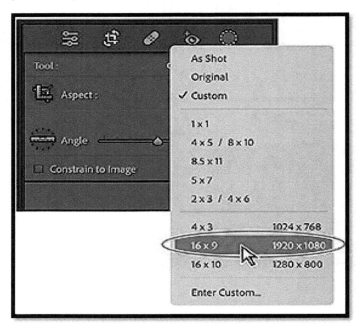

Seeing your crop better

When you crop, make sure the Lightroom window is closed. The best way to do this on a computer is to press **Shift+Tab.** The panels, Module Picker, and Filmstrip will then be covered, giving you more room for your picture.

Once the screens are hidden, press the **L** key twice. When you press the L key for the first time, Lightroom will switch to Lights Dim mode. The screen is 80% less bright in this mode. When you press the L key again, the lights go out. When you move the crop, this gets rid of the extra stuff around the edges so you can see the parts of the picture you want to change.

Because editing doesn't erase what you've done, you can use the size Overlay tool again at any time to change the photo's size or angle. Live means that you can see the parts of the picture that were cropped again. You can also flip the picture or move, resize, or crop the cropping rectangle however you want.

Press the **L** key to turn the lights back on when you're done with your crop. To get the panels back, press **Shift+Tab.**

Rotate or flip a photo in the Develop module

- Go to **Photo > Rotate Left** or Rotate Right to turn a picture 90 degrees. You can turn the picture around its center either clockwise or backward.
- Pick **Photo > Flip Horizontal** from the menu to turn a picture from front to back across the page, like a mirror. Things that were on the left are now on the right, and vice versa. It will look like the text in the picture is backward.
- To make a picture look like a mirror turned upside down, move it from front to back by choosing **Photo > Flip Vertical.**

Using the retouch and spot removal tool

Retouch Tool:

This is the Retouch tool in Adobe Lightroom Classic. It lets you get rid of big flaws or things you don't want in your pictures.

- Put the picture you want to edit into Adobe Lightroom Classic after you open it.
- There is a Develop tab in the top right corner of the screen. To get to it, click on it. Keep in mind that this will lead you to the Develop option.
- The Spot Removal tool can be found in the file on the right. You can click on it or press the **Q** key on your keyboard to use it.

250

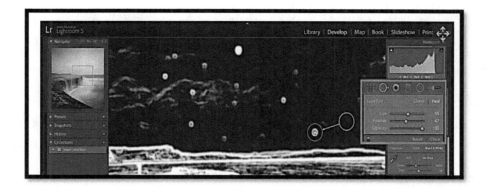

- When you want to change the size of the brush, press the [and] keys on your keyboard or drag the scale in the toolbar. That is up to you and how bad the mistake is that you want to fix.

- Before you can change something, you have to click on it. In the nearby area, Lightroom will choose a spot on its own to take a sample from.

- In case the automatic pick doesn't work out well, you can also move the starting point yourself to a better spot.

- Press the **Enter** key on your keyboard or click the **Done** button in the menu when you're done with the editing.

Spot Removal Tool :

With the Spot Removal tool, you can get rid of small flaws on the surface of something. These flaws could be dust spots or something else.

- Press the **Q** key or pick the **Spot Removal** tool in the Develop menu.

- Press the **[** and **]** keys on your keyboard or use the slider in the menu to change the size of the brush. Then, find the size of the place you want to remove.

- You have to click on the mistake to pick it up and fix it. So, Lightroom will choose a close area to use as a replacement on its own.

- You can move the starting point by hand to a better place that fits the goal if you need to.

- To save your changes, press **Enter** or click the **Done** button in the menu.

- If you find any mistakes or trouble spots in the picture, go through the steps again.

- Click on the **Z** key or the zoom tool to see the picture better and get rid of any spots.

- To take back the changes you made, press **Ctrl + Z** (on Windows) or **Cmd + Z** (on Mac). To undo changes, you could also press **Ctrl + Y** (on Windows) or **Cmd + Y** (on Mac).

You can fix a part of an image in Lightroom Classic by using a sample from another part of the same image. One way to improve a picture of scenery is to get rid of anything that doesn't belong, like people, electrical lines, and so on.

Using the Spot Removal tool

1. Press **Q** or pick the **Spot Removal** tool from the list of tools in the Develop mode.

2. Please choose one of these:

   Heal; lets you match the material, lighting, and coloring of the sampled area to the area you want to heal.

   Clone; copies the part of the picture that was sampled in the area that was picked.

3. When you drag the Size bar in the tool's options area, you can change the size of the area that it works on.

   Note: Scrolling up or down will change the tool's outline. The following keys on your computer will let you change the size of the brush:

   - If you remove this left bracket ([), the tool radius will be smaller.
   - More space around the tool is made by the right bracket (]).

4. Move your mouse over the part of the picture you want to fix.

- A white marquee spot shows you which option you want.
- There is a white frame with an arrow pointing to the pick that shows the area that was tested.

Choose the person or something else you want to clean, and then use the Spot Removal tool to paint it. Use the pins (shown on the right) to move the sample or the areas you've picked.

5. You can do one of the following to change the sampled area that is picked by default:

- **Automatically:** Press the **slash key (/)**, and the handle of a place you've picked will be clicked automatically. Someone looks at a new place. Press the forward slash key over and over until you find a good sample spot.

- **Manually:** Move the tested area's handle to a new spot and pick it out by hand.

Note: When you use longer strokes to pick out larger parts of a picture, the right sample area match is not found right away. When you click the forward slash (/), the tool will automatically take samples from more places. This lets you try out different options.

6. To take back all the changes you made with the Spot Removal tool, click the **Reset** button below the tool strip.

Keyboard shortcuts and modifiers

Circular spot:

- You can make a circle spot with just one click, and the computer will find a source on its own.

- Click and hold down **Control or Command** to make a circle-shaped spot. You can move the spot around by dragging it.

- To make a circle, hold down **Command** or **Control** and **Option** or **Alt** and click around it. You can drag the circle to change its size.

Delete a selected area or spot:

- To get rid of the change, pick out a pin and press **Delete**.

- Press **Option** or **Alt** and click on something to get rid of it.

- Press and hold the **Alt** or **Option** key while moving the mouse. This will make a marquee. Any spots inside the sign will be erased right away.

Cleaning up a photo with the Visualize Spots feature

There are some problems that you might not have seen on the computer screen that might show up when you print the picture at full quality. A picture can have flaws like dust on the sensor, spots on the person's skin, or very small clouds in a clear sky. These flaws can be annoying when seen at full size.

With the Visualize Spots tool, you can see these mistakes and fix them before you print.

It is possible to see the spots and use the scale below the picture when the Spot Removal tool is selected. If you select Visualize Spots, the picture is turned upside down to make flaws stand out more. The contrast can be changed with this tool so that flaws can be seen in more or less detail. After that, you can get rid of things that are in the way with the **Spot Removal tool** .

1. Pick the Spot Removal tool from the list of tools. Check the box next to Visualize Spots from the menu.

You can see the edges of the things in the shot because it is backward.

The left side of Visualize Spots is not turned on. The Spot Removal tool can clean up more data when you select the Visualize Spots option (on the right). Because of this, you can see the dust spots on the hat in the photos better.

2. You can change how different parts of a picture look with the Visualize Spots slider. Moving the dial to different contrast levels lets you see flaws like dust, dots, and other things you don't want to see.

3. The Spot Removal tool can be used to fix up parts of the picture. If you want to see the picture, uncheck the box that says Visualize Spots.

4. Keep repeating steps 2 and 3 until you're satisfied.

How to use presets and profiles

Presets

One set of settings can be saved so that you can use it on other pictures. You can make a setting that stays in the Develop module's Presets panel until you delete it. These settings can also be found in the list of Develop settings. When you add pictures, you can use these settings.

Preview and apply a Develop preset

The program comes with a list of presets that can be used in the Develop section. If you click on the Lightroom Classic settings folder, you can see the basic settings.

1. You can see how a preset will look on your picture by moving your mouse over it.

2. To use a preset, click on it.

The following tools are ready for you to use:

- The Preset Amount slider lets you change how strong the preset is that is being used.

- When you make or change a setting, you can turn on the Amount slider. When you open the New Develop Preset or Update Develop Preset box, click on the Support Amount Slider. If this option is not picked, the Amount slider for that setting will be grayed out.

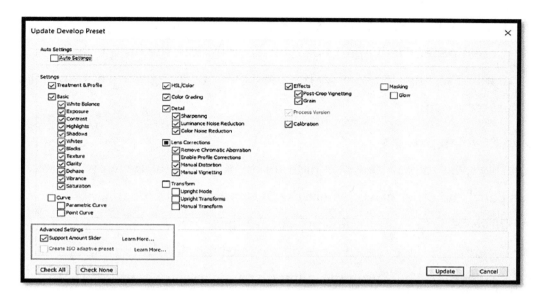

- If you can't find the Support Amount Slider option, it means that the choices you picked don't work with the Amount Slider.

- When you change sliders that aren't linked to the preset, the preset choice stays the same.

  Tip: You can sort Presets and Preset groups by name if you know how to use the Presets gallery.

Import Develop presets

Note: You can load many XMP setups and profiles, DCP profiles, and LCP profiles at once by using a zip file. There is no way to bring in .lrtemplate settings with a zip file, though.

To add Develop Presets to Lightroom Classic, do any of the following:

- Click the **plus sign (+)** in the upper right corner of the Develop module's Presets panel. Then, choose Import Presets from the list that presents itself. If the import box shows up, pick one of the preset files or a.zip file with settings inside it. When you press OK, all the presets are put into the User Presets group.

- If you want to import a preset group, right-click on it in the Develop module's Presets panel. The import box will show up. Pick the preset files or a.zip file that has settings. As soon as you press OK, the changes are put to the chosen preset group.

Manage Develop presets

Manage Presets lets you show or hide different groups of Develop presets in the Presets panel and other places where the Develop presets list appears.

Follow these steps to show or hide pre-set groups:

1. To add a preset, open the Develop module and click the plus sign (+) in the top right corner. Then, from the menu that appears, pick Manage Presets.

2. In the Manage Presets window, pick the groups of presets you want to see. Check the boxes next to the pre-set groups that you don't want to see.

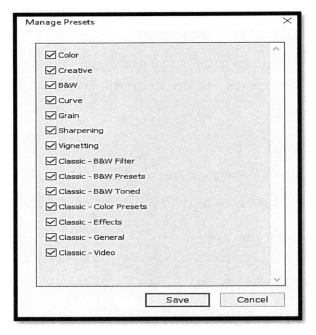

3. Click the **Save** button to save it.

   Now, the Manage Presets box only shows the groups of presets that you picked in the Presets panel.

For Windows users, right-click (or control-click) on any group of presets in the Presets box. Then, choose Reset Hidden Presets from the menu that appears. This will show you all the hidden preset groups.

Create a Develop preset

The presets you make depend on how the photo you picked is set up at the moment.

1. In the Develop section, go to the **Presets** panel and click the **plus sign (+)** in the upper right corner. You can choose **Create Preset** from the screen that comes up, or you can go to **Develop > New Preset.**

2. To add everything, click Check All. Click Check None to leave out everything. After that, click on each setting to add it to the setup.

3. Type a name for the setting in the setting Name box. Then pick a folder and click **Create**.

You added the setting to the list in the folder you picked in the Presets bar.

Create an ISO adaptive preset

Make a preset based on the ISO level of your pictures. To make an ISO adaptive preset, you need to pick at least two shots with different ISO levels. This ISO flexible preset finds the best value for the setting based on the values in the preset. If you use it on a picture that has a different ISO value, it will figure out what the right value is.

One picture with ISO 400 and Luminance Noise Reduction set to 0 and the other with ISO 1600 and Luminance Noise Reduction set to 10 will be used to make a preset. When you use that preset on an ISO 800 picture, the Luminance Noise Reduction will be set to 5.

1. Get at least two pictures with various ISO numbers. This is how you'll make the setting.

2. Any changes you need to make to these pictures should be made in the Develop section. Say you want to use a different Luminance Noise Reduction number for each ISO picture.

3. To add these pictures, click on them and then click the **plus sign (+)** in the upper right corner of the Presets board. If you'd rather not use the menu, you can go to Develop > New Preset.

4. Next, pick the choices you want to add to the new preset. Then, click **Create** at the bottom of the text box. A setup that adapts to ISO will be made.

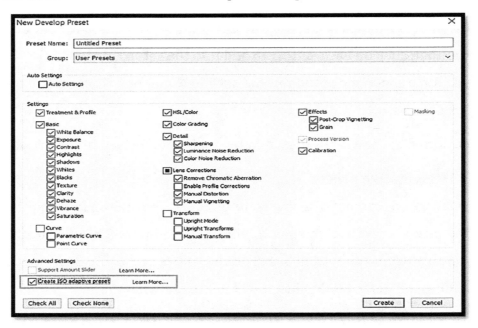

You can choose which folder to put the preset in, and it will be added to the list there.

Update a Develop preset

1. There is a user setup that you can pick from and change the settings as needed.

2. It's easy to get to a setting. Just right-click (Windows) or control-click (Mac OS) on it. After that, choose **Update With Current Settings.**

3. Pick out the changes you want to keep as a default, then click **Update**.

Export a custom preset

Lightroom Classic options and preset groups can't be sent to other programs. Only the settings that you choose can be sent.

1. Go to the **Presets panel** in the Develop module and choose a user or third-party preset that you want to share.

2. Press and hold the setting (Windows) or right-click (Mac OS) and select **Export**.

3. Pick a name for the file, then click **Save**.

Note:

- For Windows users, right-click on the preset group and choose Export Group from the menu that comes up. If you're using Mac OS X, press (Control-click) and do the same thing.

- Only the custom or third-party themes are used when the Favorite group is shared. This is still true even if the Favorite group has Lightroom Classic themes already installed.

Delete a custom preset

There is no way to get rid of the themes that come with Lightroom Classic. To get rid of custom settings is the only way.

1. In the Develop section, go to the **Presets panel** and choose **a preset**. On Windows, right-click it or press and hold it on Mac OS X, and then choose **Delete**.

   Note: Do not press the Delete key on your computer, or the picture you have chosen will be erased.

   Profiles

   Picture quality, brightness, and sharpness are all changed by the camera when you shoot in JPEG mode. When you shoot in raw mode, your camera saves both a small JPEG sample and all the raw data. This JPEG example is shown on the LCD screen on the back of the camera. It has been given color, contrast, and sharpening.

As soon as you open this picture in Lightroom, the JPEG sample shows up as a thumbnail. It starts to turn the raw data into pictures on the screen that you can see and work with. Demosaicing is the word for this. Lightroom looks at the picture's data, like the white balance and all the color settings on your camera, and tries to figure out what it all means.

It's not always the same as the JPEG you saw on the back of your camera because Lightroom doesn't understand some camera settings. You can now understand why your pictures changed color right after (or while) coming in.

Camera profiles are presets that try to copy the settings in a camera's JPEGs. This change made a lot of photographers unhappy before the makers of Lightroom added them. Not quite right, but they're close to what you saw on the camera's back. They used to be on the screen where you set up the camera.

As more shooters began to use them, some photographers made profiles with artistic effects. To give users more color accuracy and freedom in their work, Adobe knew that users would want to add profiles first, so they put them at the top of the Basic panel.

Profiles in Lightroom

Lighting Room Classic has several camera profiles in three groups that shooters can use in their work:

- **Adobe Raw profiles**: Adobe Raw profiles are profiles that can be used with photos from any camera. They're meant to make pictures look and feel more like each other.

- **Camera Matching profiles:** These profiles look like the ones that came with your camera, but they're not the same for every brand.
- **Creative profiles:** These are made for being creative, and they use Lightroom's 3D LUT tool to add even more color effects.

TIP: LUTs, which stand for color lookup tables, change the way colors look in a picture. LUTs were first used in video to try to make footage from different sources look like it came from the same source. When people started using Photoshop to add color to their pictures, they became more well-known. When used in movies, these techniques are also known as cinematic color grading.

Now that we know what these tools can do, let's look at how to use them to make our work stand out. Let's use the rider shot that we cut out again. After moving between modules, press the **D** key to make sure you are back in the Develop module. To close the left windows and the Filmstrip, press the gray squares in the middle of them. You will be able to see the changes we are making better now.

It is right below the Treatment space at the very top of the Basic panel. With the left-hand Profile menu, you can quickly get to some Adobe Raw profiles that look like how your camera is set up. When you work on a raw file, these traits are the only ones that show up. From the Profile Browser, you can also add your best profiles to this menu. This will make it easy to get to them.

NOTE: You can see the Adobe Standard V2 color profile in the list; this was the standard color profile before Lightroom 2013.

You can find the Profile Browser button on the right. It looks like four dots. You can get to different profiles from here, like the Adobe Raw Profiles.

NOTE: If you made a picture with a camera setting, like Monochrome, Lightroom will now use that picture by default. Many people are used to having their black-and-white raw pictures turned back into color ones right away. It's not going to happen in this form.

Adobe Color: This is the new way to make color pictures. It makes them look bland, like a picture you took with your camera.

Adobe Monochrome: This has been fine-tuned to be a great place to start with any black-and-white picture. Photos that were first made in Adobe Standard and then turned black and white have better contrast and color separation.

Adobe Portrait: You can change how different skin tones look more with Adobe Portrait, which is made to work best with all skin tones. It's easier to get a good headshot when you use less contrast and saturation on the skin tones across the whole picture.

Adobe Landscape: As the name suggests, was made for landscape photos, with brighter colors for the sky and leaves.

Adobe Vivid: Gives you a bright, full-color base.

There are some great Adobe Raw profiles, but most shooters will want to go straight to the Camera Matching profiles. If you want to use the profiles that come with your camera, these are the ones that were made for it. Click on the Profile Browser button to do this.

Using the Profile Browser

The Profile Browser lets you see all Adobe's profiles. We already talked about the Adobe Raw profiles that are at the top of the Profile Browser. There are profiles for your camera brand that are only found in the Camera Matching profiles. This means that the kind of camera you have will determine how many accounts you can use.

The entries for artists are at the bottom of the Profile Browser. You can sort them by style: artistic, black and white, modern, and vintage. To see how each picture will look on your photo, click on it once and then click on it again.

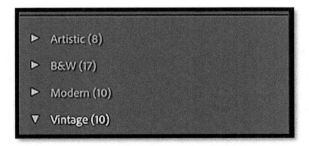

It's a good idea to try out every character. With just one click, the Camera Matching profiles might help you get closer to what you saw on the back of your camera. The Creative profiles, on the other hand, might help you see your picture in a new way.

You can fine-tune the look to your liking with the Amount slider in the artistic profiles. To return to the Basic panel, press the Close button in the upper right corner of the browser after choosing a profile and an amount setting.

They also have black-and-white presets that can make your shot better and give you a great place to start when you want to make interesting black-and-white pictures.

How to make basic adjustments to your photos

If you want to make simple changes to your photos in Adobe Lightroom Classic that will make them look better, you need to follow these steps. Here's a quick guide on how to make changes:

1. **Import Your Photo:**

   Open Lightroom Classic and add the picture you want to change.

2. **Navigate to the Develop Module:**

   Click on the Develop button in the top right corner.

3. **Basic Panel:**

   You can find the Basic panel on the right side of the Develop section.

4. **Adjust Exposure:**

   Use the Exposure tool to change how bright your picture is in general.

   To make any changes you need, use the Highlights, Shadows, Whites, and Blacks buttons.

5. **White Balance:**

   Click **White Balance** to get the right color temperature.

   The eyedropper tool can be used to find the right color. Just click on a neutral spot.

6. **Contrast and Presence:**

   Change Contrast to make the dark and light colors stand out more.

Play with Vibrance to change how strong the colors are and Clarity to change how different the mid-tones are.

7. **Tone Curve:**

You can use the Tone Curve to make more complicated changes to the tone.

8. **Detail Panel:**

Small changes should be made to Sharpening and Noise Reduction in the Detail area.

9. **Lens Corrections:**

You can fix chromatic aberration and lens distortion in the Lens Corrections panel if you need to.

10. **Crop and Straighten:**

Use the Crop Overlay tool to cut out parts of your picture and fix them.

11. **Graduated and Radial Filters:**

To make certain changes, check out the Graduated and Radial Filters. One way to change the sky is to use a Graduated Filter.

12. **Adjustment Brush:**

Use the Adjustment Brush to make little changes. You could, for instance, make some parts lighter, like faces, or darker, like bothersome parts.

13. **Presets:**

There are settings in Lightroom that you can use to make quick changes. It comes with themes, but you can also make your own and load them.

14. **Preview Before/After:**

Press the \ key to quickly go between the first and changed versions.

15. **Export Your Photo:**

Pick the picture in the Library section, then export it when you're done. Remember that these are only the most basic steps. How well the changes work will depend on how the shot was made. Don't be afraid to try new things and write the way you want to. Because Lightroom doesn't delete changes you make to photos, you can always go back and make them even better.

Using a Texture Slider

It was first thought of as a way to help with picture editing by making the skin look smoother. One way to think of it is as a more subtle way to add details (or frequency) to a part of a picture.

Picture levels are made up of high, medium, and low, so think about that. You always change the edges of things in a picture when you change something about it, like making it better. There are a lot of high frequencies in these parts of the picture. The changes will show up in the main tones and shadows of a picture if you make them too much.

It is possible to add this information to the picture's middle frequencies by moving the Texture slider. But it doesn't change the low sounds.

Clarity does a good job of making the middle tones stand out more, but it also changes a lot of other parts of the picture. It looks a bit like adding clarity when you add depth to a picture. You'll notice, though, that the details give you all the good things they do without any of the bad things that come with too much clarity.

Here's a general idea of how to use the Texture slider:

1. **Open Your Image:**

    Open the picture in Lightroom and go to the Develop tab.

2. **Find the Texture Slider:**

    For the Detail panel, go to the Develop section and look for it. In that area, you'll find the Texture scale and other tools for sharpening and lowering noise.

3. **Adjust the Texture Slider:**

    To make medium-sized features stand out, move the Texture tool to the right. This will add more texture.

This will make the picture look smoother by lowering the texture. Move the Texture tool to the left.

4. **Fine-Tune Other Settings:**

After moving the Texture tool, you may need to change other settings in the Detail panel, such as Sharpening and Noise Reduction, to get the look you want.

5. **Use in Combination:**

To make the effect more interesting, move the Texture slider and change other settings such as Clarity and Dehaze.

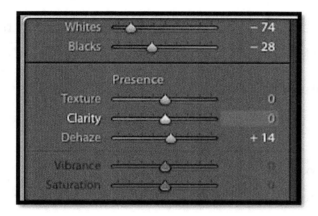

6. **Apply Locally if Needed:**

You can change the look of only some parts of a picture with the Adjustment Brush or the Graduated Filter. This lets you paint over or change the texture of only certain places.

7. **Preview Changes:**

Use the Before/After view or press and hold the **backslash (/)** key to see how the Texture scale changed things before you save your work.

Keep in mind that the Texture slider will only work with the picture you use it on and the artistic goals you set for it. You can add or take away color with this powerful tool. A lot of changes should be made until you get the look you want for your pictures.

CHAPTER 16

INTEGRATION WITH PHOTOSHOP

Round-tripping between Lightroom and Photoshop

It's helpful to switch between Lightroom and Photoshop because it lets you use the best parts of both programs to make your shots better. Here are the steps you need to take to quickly switch between these two Adobe programs:

1. **Start in Lightroom**

    Import and Organize: If you want to organize your pictures, you can bring them into Lightroom and use its strong library management tools.

    Basic Adjustments: In Lightroom, make the first changes, such as brightness, white balance, cropping, and basic color fixes. You can undo these changes at any time.

2. **Edit in Photoshop**

    Open in Photoshop: To change a picture in Adobe PhotoShop, right-click on it in Lightroom and choose **Change In > Adobe PhotoShop**. This will open the picture in PhotoShop as a smart object with the changes made in Lightroom still there.

    Advanced Edits: In Photoshop, you can fix things, use layers and masks, and do other advanced editing jobs. Photo Shop's tools are better for making deep and complicated changes.

    Save and Return to Lightroom: When you're done making changes, save the picture by going to **File > Save** in Photoshop. You can keep making changes in Lightroom even after you've saved the picture you've changed.

3. **Back in Lightroom**

    Refine Adjustments: You can make more changes to the picture in Lightroom after saving the changes you made in Picture Shop. You can make more changes without affecting the changes you made in Photoshop because the changes you make in Lightroom don't delete anything.

    Export and Share: When you're happy with the picture, you can print it or send it to someone else.

Tips for a Smooth Workflow

Use Smart Objects: You can make changes to a picture in Lightroom after opening it as a smart object in Photoshop. Then you can save the file again in Photoshop.

Preserve Layers: Remember to save your layers when you move a picture from Photoshop to Lightroom. Choose a file type like PSD or TIFF that keeps layers so you can easily make changes to the image.

Stay Organized: Use Lightroom collections and tags to keep track of which photos have been changed in Photoshop.

Use Photoshop with Lightroom Effectively

How do I access Photoshop from Lightroom?

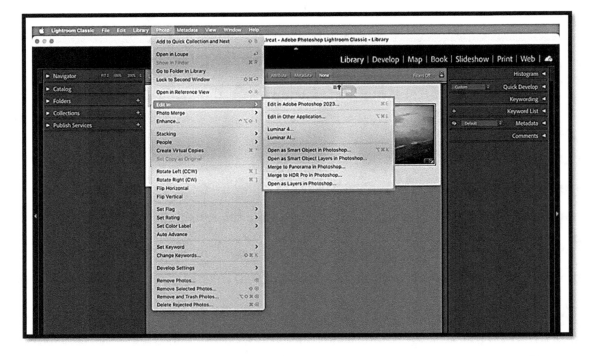

Lightroom Classic is probably what you use to edit pictures and organize files. But LRc doesn't let you do all of these things.

The work that Lightroom did is done, but you might want to clean up or do more advanced editing later.

You will need an editor with tools for changing pictures, like Adobe Photoshop, to do this. This is the reason Lightroom lets you send pictures to Photoshop right away. That's right, you won't have to export your files again.

You can change the pictures in any way you want, or you can do certain things with them, like make an HDR or PCB.

Edit In

Photoshop is still where you can work on your photos even if you only use Lightroom to manage your files or make small changes.

To do this, go to **Adobe Photoshop** and click on **Photo > Edit In > Edit**. This will open the picture that has been changed in Photoshop.

You can also right-click on the picture and do this. Then, pick **Edit In > Edit in Adobe Photoshop** from the list that appears. This works in both the Library and the Develop section.

Remember that Adobe Camera Raw won't be used when you work with raw files. The Adobe Camera Raw panel shows up when you open raw shots in Photoshop, so this is important. Plus, this way you can change the picture before you go to Photoshop.

This won't happen if you send raw files from LR to PS. Before it was sent, Lightroom had already opened the raw file and developed it.

Open as a Smart Object

A Smart Object is a unique part of Photoshop that lets you change something without affecting the original. You can make a Smart Object out of any picture in Photoshop. But you can open the picture you took in Lightroom right away in Photoshop as a Smart Object. This makes the work go faster and better.

To do this, start Photoshop and go to **Photo > Edit In > Start as a Smart Object.**

Open as Smart Object Layers

It's possible that you already know that Photoshop has layers. After that, you can put different parts of the same picture on top of each other. You can open several pictures in LR as Smart Object layers if you want to make one picture out of them.

Pick the pictures you want to use from the Library. Then, open Photoshop and go to **Photo > Edit In > Open as a Smart Object Layers.**

For each picture, a new Photoshop file will open. It's possible to make changes to one picture at a time since they are all on separate Smart Object layers.

Merge to Panorama

There is a tool in Lightroom that lets you put together several pictures into one. You can't change this feature in a lot of ways, though. Instead, Photoshop makes it easier for you to do the job.

You can use a tool to move the pictures from Lightroom to Photoshop. First, choose the pictures you want to use. Next, open Photoshop and go to **Photos > Edit In > Merge to Panorama**.

This will open the tool in Photoshop that lets you change views. They are already there in the Source Files area after you picked them out in Lightroom.

Now is the time to start the process and make changes. When it is done, the picture will show up in Photoshop.

Merge to HDR Pro

High Dynamic Range (HDR) lets you combine photos that were taken in various conditions after the fact. You'll get the most information in the blacks and highlights this way, even in scenes with a lot of contrast.

There is an HDR tool in Lightroom, and you can add plug-ins to make it even better. HDR Pro in Photoshop has more advanced tools.

You can choose which photos to mix in Lightroom. Select **Photos**, then **Edit In**, and then **Merge to HDR Pro** to open them in HDR Pro.

Open as Layers

You already know that Smart Object layers let you open more than one picture in Photoshop at the same time. You can open them as layers with raster pictures as well. To do this, open Photoshop and click on **Photo > Edit In > Open as Layers.** Don't forget to use layers when you change to keep everything. If you work on the picture layer, the source file will change.

CHAPTER 17

ADVANCED EDITING AND TONE CONTROL

Digital Negative (DNG) is a free and open standard for storing raw camera files. It was made because there wasn't an open standard. You can change raw files to DNG in Lightroom. If the original private format goes away in the future, this will still let you get to your raw files.

Making the change from RAW files to DNG (Digital Negative) files in Lightroom Classic is very simple. DNG is an open standard for RAW files that saves all of the raw data and metadata in a single file. It was created by Adobe. Here's how to change RAW files to DNG files in Lightroom Classic:

1. **Bring in RAW files:**

    In Lightroom Classic, bring in the RAW pictures that you want to turn into DNG files.

    Pick the pictures you want to change in the Library section.

2. **Go to the Library Module:**

    To get to the Library module, click on the **Library tab** in the top left corner.

3. **Choose the pictures you want to convert:**

    In the Library area, choose the photos you want to save as DNG files. Press **Ctrl** (Windows) or **Command** (Mac) to pick out more than one picture.

4. **Click on the Library menu:**

    Click **Convert Photo to DNG**... in the Library menu at the top of the screen.

5. **Set DNG Conversion Options:**

    - A dialog box called Convert Photo to DNG will show up.
    - You can change several settings here for the DNG conversion:
      - **Location:** Pick a spot to keep the changed DNG files.
      - **File Handling:**

- *Copy as DNG:* Make a copy of the original RAW file in DNG format.
- *Convert to DNG:* Put the DNG file in place of the original RAW file.
    - **Embed Fast Load Data:** Add fast load data to make DNG files load faster.
    - **Embed Original Raw File:** Back up your work by including the original RAW file inside the DNG.
    - **Compatibility:** Pick the DNG file format version.

6. **Click Convert:**

   Click **Convert** when you're done making your decisions.

7. **Wait for the conversion:**

   Lightroom Classic will turn the RAW files you pick into DNG files. The work will be shown in the app's Library section.

8. **Look at the Outcomes:**

   The new DNG files will be in the spot you picked after the change is made. You can work on these DNG files even after you turn on Lightroom Classic.

Additional Tips:

- Before you change your RAW files to DNG, make sure you have a copy of the originals. It is very important to do this if you want to replace the source files.
- Sometimes, it's easier to store pictures in DNG files. These files can have information and previews that make them easier to move around.

The DNG file format may be more useful in some cases than the RAW file format. It's also very helpful to be able to store things for a long time and share them between apps.

Understanding tone curve adjustments

You need to know how to change the tone curve in Lightroom Classic to learn how to fine-tune the color range in your photos. The Tone Curve is a powerful tool that lets you change how bright and dark your shots are. This will help you understand tone curve changes and make good ones:

1. **Tone Curve Basics:**

   The Tone Curve in Lightroom Classic is a curve that shows how the different tones in your picture are spread out. Tones that were changed (output) and those that were not changed (input) are connected in the graph.

2. **How to Read the Graph:**

   If you look at the Tone Curve graph, the input tones are shown on the horizontal axis, which goes from black to white. The output tones are shown on the vertical axis, which goes from darker to brighter.

   Shades are in the bottom left corner, bright spots are in the top right corner, and neutral tones are in the center.

3. **Understanding the S-Curve:**

   The standard S-curve change is often made to the tone curve. To do this, raise the highlights and lower the shadows to make a S shape.

   When you use an S-curve to increase contrast, you make highlights brighter and shades darker.

4. **How to Use the Parametric Tone Curve:**

   There are sliders in the Tone Curve panel that make up the Parametric Tone Curve. These sliders let you change the following sound areas:

   Highlights: This changes how bright the best parts of the picture are.

   Lights: This slider changes how bright the midtones are, which are the colors in between the blacks and the highlights.

   Darks: This slider changes how bright the darker midtones are.

   Shades: This option changes how dark parts of the picture are.

5. **Using the Point Curve:**

    To get a better handle on the Point Curve, you can move individual points on it:

    Adding Points: Click on the curve to add points.

    Dragging Points: You can move points up or down to change the brightness of the tones.

    Creating an S-Curve: To increase contrast, bring up the highlights and bring down the shadows around the curve.

6. **Adjusting Color Channels:**

    It is possible to change one or more of the RGB channels in Lightroom Classic. You can also change the Red, Green, and Blue channels separately; this can help you mix the colors just right.

    Use the drop-down button in the Tone Curve panel to pick a channel.

7. **Fine-Tuning Certain Areas:**

    Pick out certain groups of tones with the Tone Curve. With the Point Curve, you can change the colors to make the sky brighter without changing anything else in the picture.

    How to use Lightroom Classic's tone curve takes some time to get good at. See what happens when you change your shots by adding new scenes, pictures, and lighting. Over time, you'll learn how to use the tone curve to make your photos look better and have a wider range of tones.

Mastering the Tone Curve

The Tone Curve Panel

The Parametric curve and the Point curve are the two types of curves in the Tone Curve panel. There are two types of curves: the Point Curve and the Tonal Curve. Both can be used to change the values of tones in a picture.

The Parametric Curve — To pick it, use the icon that runs across the top of the Tone Curve box.

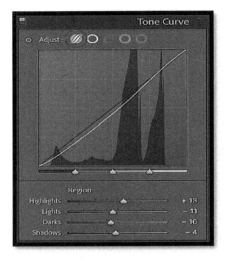

- Click and drag the **Parametric curve** up or down to change the brightness of the picture. For Highlights, Lights, Darks, and Shadows, you can also use the buttons below the curve.

- To change the range of tones that each of these sliders effects, move the shapes so that they are right under the curve.

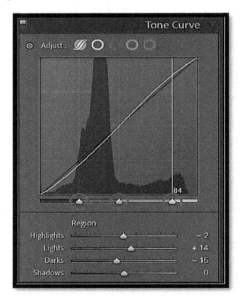

- Double-click on the name of a button to clear it. Click twice on the word **Region** to clear everything.

- Right-click (Mac) or control-click (Mac) on the **Point Curve grid** to see more options, such as Reset All, Reset Regions, Reset Splits, Reset Regions and Splits, Reset Curve, and Reset All.

- Find the light switch in the upper left area of the Tone Curve panel. Click it to show or hide changes that have been made there.

The Point Curve — Click the **dark circle** at the top of the Tone Curve box to pick the Point Curve. By adding up to 16 points, you can change the shape in small ways.

- For color changes, click on the **red, green, and blue shapes** to go to the red, green, and blue channels and make changes there. The curve shows color patterns when only one channel is picked. This helps you figure out what changes will be made.

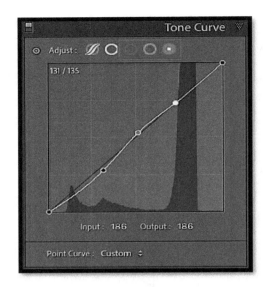

- You can change the value of any control point you choose in the input/output text boxes. This gives you more accurate control. A control point can also be moved over with the up and down arrow keys to make the change even more accurate.

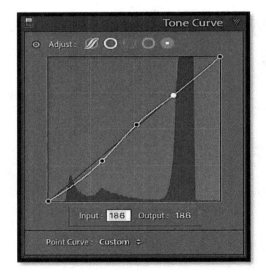

- To get rid of a point on the Point Curve, click on it and drag it off the curve.
- Click twice on the words **Point Curve** to get rid of the Point Curve.

- Once you're done making the curve, click the drop-down menu to the right of Point Curve and select **Save**. This will save the curve, so you can use it on other images.

Note: The curve can be used in both Lightroom Classic and Adobe Camera Raw if you save it where it was saved first.

- You can see more options on the Point Curve grid if you control-click (Mac) or right-click (Windows) on it. These include Reset Channel, Reset All Channels, Copy/Paste Channel Settings, Snap to Grid, and Show All Curves.

Basic Tone Curve Adjustments

Lightroom Classic's Tone Curve is a strong tool that lets you change the color and contrast of your photos in lots of different ways. By changing how the color values are shown graphically, you can change the shadows, highlights, and midtones. In Lightroom Classic, here's how to make easy changes to the tone curve:

1. **In the Develop Module, open a picture:**

   To open a picture, start Lightroom Classic and go to the **Develop section.**

2. **Locate the Tone Curve Panel:**

   Most of the time, the Tone Curve Panel is on the right side of the Develop section.

3. **Understand the Tone Curve Graph:**

   Tone Curve is a graph that shows how the different tones in your picture are spread out. Upcoming tones are shown on the left side of the graph, which goes from black to white, and outgoing tones are shown on the right side, which goes from darker to brighter.

4. **Basic Tone Curve Adjustments:**

   You can change the tone curve in Lightroom Classic in two ways: with the parametric curve or the point curve.

a. **Parametric Curve (RGB):**

The tone curve can be changed with knobs on the Parametric Curve.

Highlights: Move the Highlights tool to the left to make the highlights darker. Move them to the right to make them brighter.

Lights: When you move the Lights tool, you can change the midtones.

Darks: Move the Darks tool to change the darker color tones.

Shadows: The Shaders tool lets you change how shaders are dark or light.

b. **Point Curve (RGB):**

You have more power over each point on the curve when you use the Point Curve.

Adding Points: Click on the **curve** to add points. Most of the time, a straight line means that nothing has changed.

Dragging Points: Click and drag a point to change the slope and tone levels.

S-Curve: To make the picture stand out more, make a S curve by moving the highlights and shadows up and down.

5. **Adjusting Specific Color Channels:**

What are the Red, Green, Blue, and RGB color channels? You can change them all in Lightroom Classic.

Pick a channel from the drop-down choice in the Tone Curve box. After that, make the changes.

6. **Before and After Preview:**

Press the button in the bottom left corner of the Tone Curve box to see a split view of your picture before and after the changes.

7. **Fine-Tuning Other Settings:**

   Tone curve changes are often part of a bigger editing process. You can change settings like brightness, contrast, and color after you've changed the tone curve.

8. **Experiment and Practice:**

   Change and try out different curve shapes to see how they make your picture look.

   Remember that being subtle often makes things look more casual.

9. **Resetting the Curve:**

   Find the small curve button at the bottom of the Tone Curve box and click on Linear. This will clear the tone curve.

   You have full control over the color range of your photos once you learn the Tone Curve in Lightroom Classic. This lets you give them the look and feel you want. If you use this powerful tool more and more, you will get better at it.

Using the Targeted Adjustment Tool

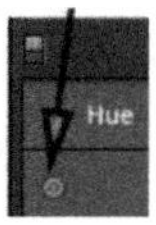

The Targeted Adjustment Tool —It's the small circle button in the upper left corner of the Tone Curve Box that you press to make changes to a specific area. You can change either the Point Curve or the Parametric Curve on the screen.

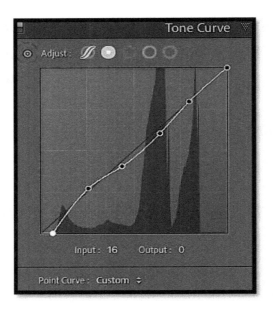

- Press **Command + Option + Shift + T** on a Mac to open the Targeted Adjustment tool. Press **Control + Alt + Shift + T** on a Windows computer to open it.

- To make changes, use the **Targeted Adjustment Tool** to click and drag the picture sample up and down.

- This tool goes back to its original state when you press **Esc**, but any changes you've made are still there.

- To make small changes with the **Targeted Adjustment tool**, move the cursor over the number you want to change in the picture preview. Then, press the up and down buttons without clicking to move the curve. You can move the point farther if you press the Shift key.

How to back up and restore your Lightroom Classic Catalog

To protect your picture library and information, you should back up and restore your Lightroom Classic catalog often. Making a backup of your changes, groups, and how the catalog is organized will let you get them back if something goes wrong with your tools or with your work. That's all you need to do to save a copy of your Lightroom Classic album and restore it.

How to Back Up Your Lightroom Classic Catalog:

1. **Startup Lightroom Classic:**

    Lightroom Classic should be open after you turn on your computer.

2. **Go to the Catalog Settings:**

    Take a look at the Catalog Settings. To do this, go to the **Edit menu** on Windows or the Lightroom Classic menu on Mac and select Catalog Settings.

3. **Navigate to the Backup Tab:**

    Look for the Backup tab in the Catalog Settings box.

4. **Choose the Backup Frequency:**

    Pick how often to back up automatically. You can choose between Once a Week and Every Time Lightroom Exits. Making regular copies is a good idea.

5. **Specify Backup Location:**

    Choose a spot to keep your files. Save them somewhere other than your main library, like on a separate hard drive.

6. **Click OK to Save Settings:**

    Click **OK** to save the changes you made to the backup settings. Please click **OK** when you are done.

7. **Manually Trigger a Backup:**

    You can start a backup by hand by going to the **File menu** and selecting **Backup Catalog**.

8. **Choose Backup Options:**

    You can pick some options in the Backup Catalog dialog box. For example, you can check Test Integrity Before Backing Up to make sure the backup is good.

9. **Press Backup:**

    Click the **Backup** button to make a backup by hand.

How to Restore Your Lightroom Classic Catalog:

1. **Locate Your Backup:** If you want to get your store back, you must first find the backup file. This copy could be one that you made or one that was made for you.

2. **Close Lightroom Classic:** Before you start the restoration, make sure Lightroom Classic is stopped.

3. **Copy the Backup:** The backup catalog file (.lrcat) should be moved from where it is being saved to where your main catalog is kept.

4. **Rename or Replace:** To save a copy of the current catalog file, rename it YourCatalogName_old.lrcat or just replace it with the copy.

5. **Startup Lightroom Classic:** Open Lightroom Classic. It will find the changes to the catalog right away and open the catalog that has been fixed.

6. **Look for Recent Changes:** Make sure that the catalog you used to back up has the most recent changes and improvements you made.

If you back up your Lightroom Classic catalog often, you can protect the important changes you make to the data, organization, and edits. Back up your library in a different location from your main library so you don't lose info if your hardware breaks or something else happens that you didn't expect.

Advanced importing techniques

Auto Import

The Auto Import feature looks for pictures in a watched folder and then adds them to a library. This can be done for a Lightroom Classic library or pack. After setting up auto-import, all you have to do to add pictures to Lightroom Classic is drag them into the watched folder. It will do the rest without you having to open the import window.

You can use Auto Import instead of Lightroom Classic if it doesn't work with your camera for connected import: You can save pictures to a folder that you watch with the software that came with your camera.

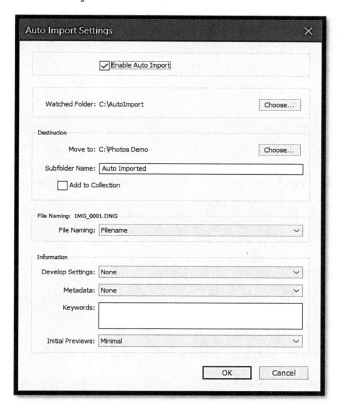

Note: Lightroom Classic will start right away when you add a camera or card reader to your computer. To stop this, go to your import preferences and change them.

Enable automatically importing photos

Click File and then Auto Import. Auto Import should be on.

Choose how to auto-import.

1. Go to **File**, then **Auto Import**, and finally **Auto Import Settings**.
2. Pick one of the following from the Auto Import Settings box:

   Watched Folder: When you open Lightroom Classic, it looks in the Watched Folder for photos to import immediately. You can pick a watched area or make one. You need to give an empty folder. Auto Import does not keep an eye on any subfolders inside a watched folder.

Destination: Choose a folder or make one to put the photos that were instantly imported in.

File Naming: File Naming lets you give the picture that was quickly imported a name.

Information: It adds settings, metadata, or keywords to pictures that were brought in instantly.

3. In the Initial Previews menu, choose Standard. This will make Lightroom Classic show previews of the photos you've imported instead of just the previews that are already in the photos.

Set up watched folders

1. In the Auto Import Settings box, choose the **Watched Folder** and press the **Choose button** next to it.

2. Go to the place you want to see and do one of these:
    o Right-click on **Make New Folder** in Windows and choose **Overwrite New Folder**. Then, give the folder a name. Go to Mac OS X and click on **New Folder.** Name the folder and then click on **Create.**
    o Pick an area that is already being looked at to choose it.
    Note: You can't watch a folder that already has pictures in it.

3. Click **OK** in Windows. Press **Choose** in Mac OS X.

Select a destination folder for auto-imported photos

Pictures added to a watched folder are moved to a target folder by Lightroom Classic when it finds them. This lets you add the pictures to a collection or the catalog.

To import photos to a catalog, do the following:

1. Click on the **Choose button** next to **Move To** in the **Destination area** of the **Auto Import Settings box.**

2. Find the place you want to go in the **Open** (Mac OS) or **Browse For Folders** (Windows) box. Then do one of these things:

   o Right-click on **Make New Folder** in Windows and choose **Overwrite New Folder.** Then, give the folder a name. Go to Mac OS X and click on **New Folder. Name the folder** and then click on **Create.**

   o Pick a folder that is already there to use it.

3. Click **OK** in Windows. Press **Choose** in Mac OS X.

4. You can name the folder in the box that says **Subfolder Name**, but you don't have to.

To import photos to a collection, do the following:

1. Check the box next to Destination that says Add to Collection. Lightroom Classic now has a drop-down menu that shows all of your Collections.

2. Pick any Collection as the spot where you want to load automatically.

3. If you want, you can click Create Collection to make a new collection and pick that as the location where the data will be brought in.

4. Press the **OK** button.

Apply Develop settings and metadata to auto-imported photos

Do any of these things in the Information part of the Auto Import Settings box:

- Please choose a preset from the page for Develop Settings to use Develop settings on photos that are sent to you instantly.

- You can add metadata to pictures that were instantly imported by using a preset from the Metadata menu.

- Type terms into the terms text box for pictures that were automatically imported. There should be commas between the words.

- You can tell Lightroom Classic to use previews of the downloaded photos instead of just the previews that are already in the photo files by going to **Initial Previews > Standard**.

CHAPTER 18

Exploring Advanced Features

How To Use The Calibration Pane

You can change the color of your image shadows by adding more pink or green. After that, you can change the major colors' hue and brightness. These are blue, green, and red. So, why do we level up? The HSL only changes the hue bands that are set for each scale. The calibration sliders, on the other hand, change the values of every pixel.

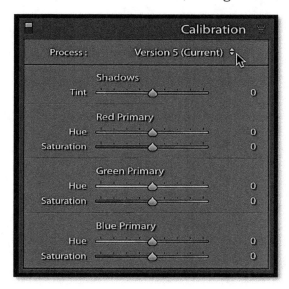

You can think of editing as setting the colors for your picture. Check out what happens by moving the buttons left and right. It can help you choose colors and where to begin with your picture. After that, you can change how strong each slider is and add your changes to the picture as normal.

It is possible to change the numbers of all the pixels in Lightroom by going to the Calibration area. To change each pixel's mix of red, green, and blue to something that might look better with the scene, the lights, or your style. You can get a Canon look with the Calibration tool, even if you don't have a Canon camera.

You can get rid of color cast in photos with the Calibration tool, which doesn't change the color of things that should stay that color.

This tool lets you change the color style a lot as well. In this case, you can change all the yellow and green colors to green.

There are no rules you have to follow when you use Adobe Lightroom's Calibration tool. Do not use it before making other color changes, though, because it can make your edit look bad.

Making all of your changes ahead of time is better. Then, when you're happy with everything, use Calibration to finish. Once you know how to use this tool, you'll be able to make your pictures look more like you.

You can make small changes to how the colors look in your photos with the Calibration panel in Lightroom Classic. Small changes to the main color bands (Red, Green, and Blue) can give it a certain look. This is how you can use the Calibration panel:

1. **Open Your Image in the Develop Module:**

   Open **Lightroom Classic** and go to the **Develop section**. After that, open the picture you want to change.

2. **Locate the Calibration Panel:**

   The Calibration Panel is in the Develop section. Most of the time, it's at the bottom of the right screen, next to where you set up the camera.

3. **Understand the Calibration Sliders:**

   In the Calibration panel, there are sliders for the main color bands of red, green, and blue. Two settings can be found on each channel:

   o   **Hue:** Hue changes the overall color tone of that channel.

   o   **Saturation:** This setting changes how bright or strong that color channel is.

4. **Adjusting the Hue and Saturation:**

   Use the tools to make small changes to the hue and saturation of the Red, Green, and Blue color channels.

- o   Swipe to the right to make the color or saturation greater.
- o   To lessen the brightness or hue, move the buttons to the left.

5. **Use as a Creative Tool:**

   The Calibration box isn't just for setting colors; it can also be used to make beautiful art. Change the sliders until your picture looks the way you want it to.

6. **Creating a Vintage Look:**

   Lowering the saturation in the Blue main channel might help if you want to make something look old or worn. You can try out different warm and cool tones by changing the color of the Red and Green channels.

7. **Achieve Consistent Color Profiles:**

   Use the Calibration box to give all of your pictures the same color profile. Changing the hue and brightness can help a group of pictures look like they all belong to the same set.

8. **Fine-Tune Skin Tones:**

   Use the Calibration box to improve the way skin tones look in pictures. To get skin tones that look good and real, you can change the Red and Green channels.

9. **Combine with Other Develop Settings:**

   You can make full changes to a picture by combining the Calibration tweaks with other Develop module settings, such as Exposure, Contrast, and Tone Curve.

Syncing Calibration Settings

- After using a setting, make any changes you think are needed to your picture, like the brightness, white balance, shadows, or anything else you think is important.

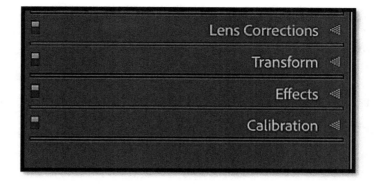

- Click on the last picture in the group while holding down the **Shift** key to choose the other pictures you want to change or make the default.

- Hold down the **Control** key and click on the pictures you want to sync. If they aren't already together, do this.

- Go to the bottom right part of the screen and click on the **Sync** button. It's next to the Edit Panels.

- For those who DO NOT WANT TO SYNC ALL THE CHANGES, click the **Check None button** to remove all of the choices. Then, check the boxes next to the changes you DO WANT TO SYNC and click Synchronize.

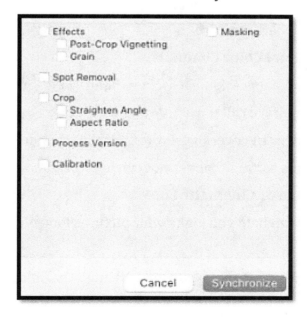

Tips and tricks for using the Calibration pane

Lightroom Classic has a great tool called Calibration that is easy to forget about. It lets you make small changes to how the colors in your photos react. To get a certain look and fine-tune the color rendering, it works especially well. To get the most out of the Calibration panel, here are some tips:

1. **Understanding the Calibration Panel:**

    Calibration is the name of the panel in the Develop section where you can find it.

    It lets you change the shades of red, green, and blue in your picture.

2. **Use It as a Creative Tool:**

    That's right, you can make things with the Calibration box as well as fix them. Moving the buttons around will give you different color effects that you can use in your art.

3. **Fine-Tune Color Balance:**

    You can make small changes to the color balance of your picture in the Calibration panel. For example, you can make small changes to skin tones or the overall color temperature.

4. **Modify Individual Color Channels:**

    There are two changes for each color band (Red, Green, and Blue) in the Calibration panel. We call these Hue and Saturation.

    Hue: This changes the overall color tone of that channel.

    Saturation: This setting changes how vivid or bright a color is.

5. **Achieve Vintage or Cinematic Looks:**

    These settings can help you make your pictures look old or like they belong in a movie.

    To make something look worn or old, change the colors and turn down the brightness.

6. **Correct Color Casts:**

   Use the Calibration box to fix pictures that have too much or too little color. To make things look more even, you can change the numbers that go with a color if you think it is too strong or not strong enough.

7. **Create Consistent Color Profiles:**

   You can make color settings that work for all your pictures in the Calibration panel so that a bunch of pictures look the same.

8. **Use It in Conjunction with Other Develop Settings:**

   This module's Calibration screen is not the only thing that makes it up. Along with choices like Exposure, Contrast, and Tone Curve, it can be used to completely change a picture.

9. **Apply It to Specific Areas with Local Adjustments:**

   If you only want to change certain parts of your picture, use local adjusting tools like the Graduated Filter, the Radial Filter, or the adjusting Brush.

10. **Create Presets for Consistency:**

    Once you find a Calibration setting you like, you should save it. You can give different pictures the same color look this way.

11. **Toggle Before and After:**

    Press the **Y/Y (Before/After)** button in the bottom left corner of the screen to go between the original and changed versions of your picture.

12. **Export with Consideration for Color Space:**

    When you send your pictures, be sure to pay attention to the color space you pick. Adobe RGB and ProPhoto RGB have wider color ranges than sRGB, which is good for printing colors.

13. **Regularly Calibrate Your Monitor:**

    So that you can use the Calibration panel correctly, make sure that your monitor is set up correctly.

You can change things in Lightroom Classic's Calibration box. Don't be afraid to move the buttons around until you find the right color tones. You can change a lot about how your pictures look and feel with this tool.

Understanding the Sliders

The Develop section of Lightroom Classic has a lot of sliders that you can use to make small changes to your pictures. You can change the color, brightness, exposure, and more with each slider. Here is a list of important Lightroom Classic settings and what they do:

The basic panel:

1. **Exposure:**

   Changes how bright the picture is in general. Moving it to the left makes it less visible while moving it to the right makes it more visible.

2. **Contrast:**

   Chooses how much the picture's lightest and darkest areas stand out from each other. Things stand out more when the contrast is high, and they look flat when the contrast is low.

3. **Highlights:**

   Make the highlights in your picture less bright. Lessen to get back features in bright spots.

4. **Shadows:**

   The brightness of the shadows can be changed. Make it bigger to see things that aren't as clear.

5. **Whites:**

   Changes some parts of the picture's brightness. It helps make the white point.

6. **Blacks:**

   Changes how dark parts of the picture look. It helps make the black point.

Tone Curve Panel:

1. **Point Curve:** Moving a curve can make exact changes to the tones in a picture.

2. **Parametric Curve:** To change the tone curve, use the choices for lights, darks, highlights, and shadows.

Presence Panel:

1. **Clarity:** Brightens the middle tones so that they stand out more, giving the picture more depth. When you have good values, things become easier. When you have bad values, things become less clear.

2. **Vibrance:** Vibrance changes how bright colors are that aren't fully saturated without changing fully saturated colors.

3. **Saturation:** This setting changes how vibrant the colors are in your whole picture.

Color Panel (HSL/Color/B&W):

1. **Hue:** To change the general tone of the colors, use hue. It changes the color but not the brightness or saturation.

2. **Saturation:** This setting changes how bright a color is. To make a color stand out more, raise it; to dull it down, lower it.

3. **Luminance:** Luminance changes how bright a color is. You can turn it up or down to change the brightness.

Split Toning Panel:

1. **Highlights Hue/Saturation:** Gives color to the picture's bright spots. You can change the color by changing the hue and the brightness.

2. **Shadows Hue/Saturation:** Fills in the dark parts of the picture with color. You can change the color by changing the hue and the brightness.

Detail Panel:

1. **Sharpening:** This changes how clear it is. Do not sharpen too much, as that can lead to mistakes.

2. **Noise Reduction:** Gets rid of picture noise, especially when the ISO is high.

Lens Corrections Panel:

1. **Basic:** In basic terms, chromatic mistakes and lens distortions were fixed. Makes it possible to change your lens's profile.

2. **Manual:** You can change distortion, vignetting, and chromatic aberration by hand with this setting.

Effects Panel:

1. **Post-Crop Vignetting:** After you crop the picture, you can add a dark or light tint to the edges to shape them.

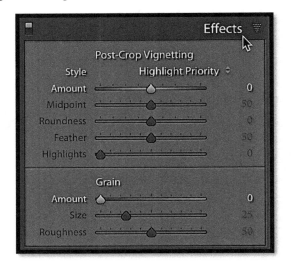

2. **Grain:** Adding film grain to a picture makes it look older.

Calibration Panel:

1. **Red Primary, Green Primary, Blue Primary:**

   Changing the mix of basic colors changes the way the colors look in the whole picture.

   You can control different parts of your picture with these sliders in Lightroom Classic. This lets you make exact changes and be creative. Try moving these buttons around and seeing how they change your pictures. This will help you understand how they work.

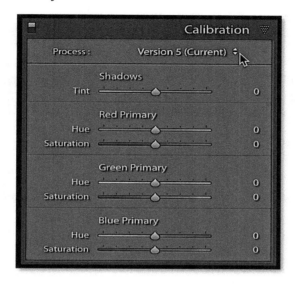

How to use the Dehaze slider

The Dehaze slider in Lightroom Classic does exactly what it says it does: it lets you add or remove mist from the air from your photos.

One of the best ways to use it is to clear up landscape shots that were taken in the fog or haze.

It's not always clear how Dehaze can be used to look good. This is interesting for creative photographers because it helps give your pictures mood and atmosphere. Adobe says that the Dehaze setting will get rid of flare and weather haze. It checks how light is spread out in a picture and tries to make things farther away look better.

Before Adobe added Dehaze, the only options were to make the contrast or clarity stronger. This effect is different and works better than the last one.

Remember that shots get darker when you move the Dehaze tool to the right. Moving the Shadows or Exposure settings to the right will fix it.

At the bottom of the Basic panel are panels that let you change your presence. One of them is the Dehaze scale.

Making changes is easy. Just tap on Dehaze and move the slider or press the - and + keys on your computer. You can quickly find the best setting by moving the Dehaze tool up and down the scale with the keyboard shortcuts. Five people work together.

The second Dehaze control is in the Masks panel, in the space for local changes. It is right next to the buttons for Texture and Clarity.

Here are the steps:

- Open **Adobe Lightroom Classic** and find the picture you want to change.

- After adding the picture, click the **Develop** tab in the upper right area to go to the Develop box.

- The right side of the Develop area has a lot of screens. Basic is where you can find the **Dehaze** option.

- Scroll down in the **Basic** panel until you reach the **Presence Section** area. Here's where the Dehaze button is.

- You can change how much dehaze you want by moving the Dehaze tool to the right or left. By making the highlights and mid-tones more or less contrasty, the tool lets you get rid of weather haze or fog in your picture.

- You might need to change more than just the Dehaze tool, depending on the picture. To get the look you want, you might need to change things like the brightness, contrast, or sharpness.

- Press and hold the **Y** key on your keyboard to see a picture of what was there before and what was thereafter. You can see how your changes have made things different.

  Most of the time, adding the Dehaze effect slowly works better than making big changes all at once. This is very important if you want the result to look real.

Advanced export options for printing and web output

Do these things to save pictures to a hard drive, a CD, or a DVD:

1. Click on the **movies** and **photos** you want to export, then press **File > Export**. By default, Lightroom Classic saves shots to the hard drive. This can be seen in the Export To menu at the top of the box.

2. Pick out the disc you want to burn by going to **Export To > CD/DVD.**

3. You can pick where to export, what to name the files, how to format them, how big and clear the images should be, what information to include, whether to add a watermark and what to do after the export.

Export location

1. You can choose where to save the file in the Export To box that appears.

2. You can select **Put In Subfolder** if you want the photos to be sent to a subfolder inside the target folder. Name the section something.

3. Select **Add To This Catalog** and check the box if you want **Lightroom Classic** to add the exported photos right away to the current collection. Select the area where the original file is saved and check the box next to **Add To Stack**. This will add the new picture on top of the old one. When you export while looking at a collection, the stack is made in the folder that holds the collection. You can only see it if you choose **As Source** or that folder.

4. Tell it what to do if there is already a file with the same name on the host:

Ask What To Do: It will show you a message asking you what to do. You can choose a new name, overwrite the current file, or choose not to export the file at all to fix the name problem.

Choose A New Name For The Exported File: As you type this command, a space, and a number are added to the end of the saved file to give it a new name.

Overwrite WITHOUT WARNING: You can overwrite a file without being told, which means that the current file is replaced with the one you're sending without any warning.

Skip: Don't send the picture anywhere else.

Pressing the **Services panel** in the **Library module** lets you save a bunch of pictures to your computer. Putting photos in a folder on your hard drive is a quick way to get them ready to be sent to an iPad or other phone or computer.

Set up a hard drive connection

Through the link to Publish Services, you can change how the export works.

1. In the **Publish Services panel** on the left side of the Library module, click the **Set Up hard drive button.**

2. There is a Publish Services Description box in the Lightroom Classic Publishing Manager that you need to fill.

3.   Give people more ways to publish.

4.   If you click on the **plus sign (+)** at the top of the **Publish Services** screen, you can always change how your hard drive is connected. You can click it and then choose **Hard Drive > Edit Settings.**

Add and manage photos in a hard drive folder

You can keep track of pictures you want to save to your hard drive in publishing collections, which are also known as files.

1.   Click the **hard drive link** in the Publish Services panel with the right mouse button (Control-click) and choose one of the choices below. This will store things on your hard drive.

   Create Published Folder

   A file where all the pictures you've chosen are saved.

   Create a Published Smart Folder

   A set of rules for how the pictures should be put together.

   Create a Published Folder Set

   A group of files that are public.

2.   Drag pictures from the Grid view to the folder you want to make in the Publish Services panel. When you make a smart box, pictures that follow your rules will be put in it straight away.

3.   To keep track of your hard drive files, do any of the following:

   o   If you want to delete a folder from the Publish Services panel, right-click (Windows) or control-click (Mac OS) on it and choose Edit Collection, Rename, or Delete. You can also change the folder's name.

   o   In a normal hard drive folder, pick out the picture you want to get rid of and press the Delete key.

   o   You can add or remove photos from a smart folder by changing its rules.

- Find the folder with the pictures in the Publish Services panel and click on it to see the pictures. The pictures are set up in the area where they are shown in the following groups or queues:
  - **New Photos To Publish:** Pictures that haven't been sent anywhere else yet.
  - **Modified Photos To Republish:** Photos that were changed in the Library or Develop section after they were exported and then republished.
  - **Published Photos:** Photos that have been published have not been changed since they were exported.
  - **Deleted Photos To Remove:** It says Deleted Photos To Remove next to photos you delete from a folder. Lightroom Classic marks these photos as Deleted Photos To Remove when you delete them. When you click Publish again, they are taken out of the folder.

Export photos to hard drive

You can see two lines of photos: New Photos To Publish and Modified Photos To Republish. It sends everything in both lines when you post a folder or set of folders.

1. To save pictures to a hard drive, you need to do one of these things:
   Pick out a place on your computer and click **Publish**.

   For Windows, right-click or control-click on a folder on your hard drive and choose **Publish Now.** Mac OS X users should do the same.

2. If asked, click **Replace** to add pictures that have already been made public in newer versions.

Best export settings for high-resolution prints

When you send photos from Lightroom Classic to make high-resolution prints, you should make sure that the settings you use to keep the picture quality and color accuracy are intact. These are the best export settings for making high-resolution copies:

1. **File Type:**

   Choose the type of file that you want to print. For high-quality prints, most people pick TIFF or JPEG with the best settings.

   TIFF, which stands for Tagged Image File Format, is a file that doesn't lose any quality when you save a picture.

   You can get away with a lot of compression flaws in a JPEG file when the quality setting is set to high.

2. **Color Space:**

   Choose the correct color space to print. Adobe RGB is often used for print work because it has a wider range of colors than sRGB.

   If your print service gives you one, use the color space they tell you to use.

3. **Bit Depth:**

   Choose 16 bits per channel to get more color information and smoother changes in tone. But it's possible that some printers can only handle 8 bits per channel.

4. **Resolution:**

   Change the resolution to the one that came with your printer or the one that your print service provider offers.

   300 pixels per inch (PPI) is a common resolution for good prints. However, different printers may need different levels of resolution.

5. **Image Sizing:**

Make your picture the right size for the paper you want to print it on. If you want to keep the numbers as they were, don't check the Resize to Fit box.

6. **Sharpening:**

Use clarity for output when you want to print. For the paper you want to print on, choose Matte Paper or Glossy Paper. The picture will be sharpened to a certain degree, depending on its size and type.

7. **Metadata:**

Check to see if the copied file has any author attribution and other useful data.

8. **File Naming and Location:**

Pick a place to save the file you just copied and give it a name that makes sense.

Export Steps in Lightroom Classic:

1. **Choose an image(s):**

You can choose the picture or pictures you want to send in the Library app.

2. **Go to the Export Dialog:**

Pick **Export** from the File menu or press **Ctrl + Shift + E** (Windows) or **Cmd + Shift + E** (Mac).

3. **Set Export Settings:**

Follow the steps above to set up the choices in the Export window.

4. **Choose Export Location:**

Pick out a location to export the files you've saved.

5. **Click on Export:**

Click the **Export** button to start the process.

Your photos will be ready to print in high quality if you use these export settings. They will have the right colors and level of sharpness. Always make sure you get clear instructions from your print service. Also, you might want to print a few to see how they come out before making a big lot.

How to work and install external editors

Under External Editing, you can make a list of your best outside editors. After that, these will show up in Photo > Edit In. That's because Photoshop will be on the list if you have it on your computer.

You can use other programs to improve your editing skills when you work with outside writers in Lightroom Classic. These steps will show you how to use outside tools and add new ones:

1. **Configure External Editors in Lightroom Classic:**

    Startup Lightroom Classic: Click on Lightroom Classic and turn on your computer.

    Go to Preferences: To do this on a Mac, open **Lightroom Classic** and select **Preferences**. Click **Edit** and then **Preferences** in Windows.

    Select the External Editing Tab: In the **Preferences** window, go to the **External Editing option**.

    Configure External Editor Settings: Choose an app from the **Additional External Editor** drop-down button. In this window, you can change the size, color space, bit level, file format, and other options for the outside editor.

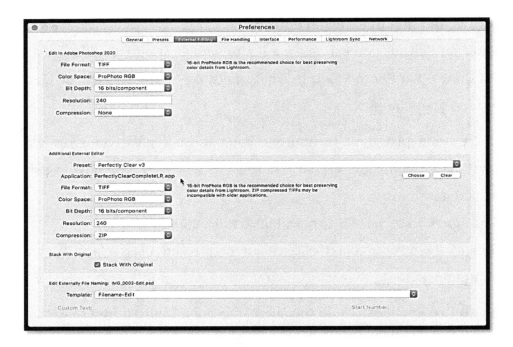

Choose Editing Options: Pick whether you want to change the original picture or a copy of it. You can also put the picture that has been changed on top of the first one.

Set File Naming: If you need to, you can change the names of the files that hold the changed pictures.

Press OK: Do not forget to press OK to save your changes when you are done setting up.

2. **Send Images to External Editors:**

    Pick out the picture(s) in Lightroom: In the **Library** or **Develop** module, choose the picture(s) you want to change.

    Right-click and choose Edit In: To change a picture, right-click on it and choose **Edit In** from the menu that comes up.

Choose External Editor: From this list, pick the external editor that you set up in Preferences. You can open the picture(s) you picked in any outside program you want.

3. **Edit in External Editor:**

   Perform Edits in External Application: To make the changes you want, use the outside editor's tools and features.

   Save the Changes: Remember to save the changes you made in the outside editor. Based on how it's set up, the changed picture may be saved as a separate file or replace the original.

   Return to Lightroom: Leave the outside editor open and go back to Lightroom. Now, the changed picture should appear in Lightroom as a new copy of the first one.

4. **Install New External Editors:**

   Download and Install External Editor: You need to get the tool and set it up on your computer to add an external editor.

   Configure External Editor in Lightroom: To set up an external editor in Lightroom, go to the **External Editing tab** in the **Lightroom Classic Preferences.**

   Choose the New Editor: In the **Additional External Editor** section, click **Choose** and locate the executable file for the new editor.

   Configure Settings: Choose the **file format, color space, bit level,** and **resolution** for the **new external editor,** among other things.

   Press OK: To save the changes you made in the outside editor, press **OK**.

   After that, if you right-click on a picture in Lightroom and choose **Edit In**, the new outside editor should appear in the list.

Advanced watermarking techniques

Create a copyright watermark

1. From anywhere in the program, go to **Edit > Edit Watermarks** (Windows) or **Lightroom Classic > Edit Watermarks** (macOS).

2. Choose a Watermark Style from the list of Text or Graphic in the Watermark Editor box.

3. Either of these things needs to be done:

   Type the text in the sample area and use the Text Options menu to change the font, style, alignment, color, and drop shadow. OpenType fonts can't be used.

   (Watermark on a picture) Click **Choose** in the Image Options pane. After that, click on the PNG or JPEG file you want to use.

4. Write down what the marking does:

   Opacity: You can change how plain the marking is or how clear it is.

Size: The relative scale changes how big the watermark is. Fit makes the label cover the whole picture. It makes the mark take up the whole picture in terms of height and width.

Inset: This feature changes the watermark around in the image, either left to right or up and down.

Anchor: The label can be moved left or right and fixed in nine different spots in the picture.

Note: If the stamp on the last picture is hard to see, try making it bigger or moving it around on the picture.

5.   Click **Save**.

Manage copyright watermarks

- If you're on Windows, go to any section and click **Edit > Edit Watermarks**. On macOS, go to **Edit Watermarks** in Lightroom Classic.

- Click the **Left** and **Right arrow buttons** to see a preview of the stamp on each picture in the **Filmstrip**. This only works if you have more than one picture selected.

- After making your choices, click **Save** to leave the **Watermark Editor** and save them as a preset. You can save the watermark by clicking the **Presets** menu in the upper left corner of the window and choosing **Save Current Settings As New Preset**. You can then continue working in the **Watermark Editor**. Type a name for the new preset and click **Create**.

- Pick a **watermark** from the menu in the upper left part of the screen.

- To change how a stamp works, choose it from the list of pre-sets. Then, go back to the preset menu and choose **Update Preset [name]**.

- Find the copyright marking you want to change the name of in the preset menu. After that, click the **menu** again and pick **Rename Preset [name].**

- Choose the **watermark** you want to get rid of from the preset options. After that, click the **menu** again and pick **Delete Preset [name]**.

CHAPTER 19

TROUBLESHOOTING AND COMMON ISSUES

Common Issues and Solutions

Adobe Lightroom Updates Issues

Before you update Adobe Lightroom, you should make a copy of your data and make sure your computer can run the latest version. Make sure that changes work well and that your work is safe.

Checking OS Compatibility

Making sure that the fix works with everything is very important. For the newest version of Lightroom, your operating system (OS) might need to meet certain standards. It's simple to check:

- **For Windows users:** If you use Windows, make sure you have at least Windows 10 (64-bit).

- **For Mac users:** If you have a Mac, your OS should be at least Mojave (18.14).

  Here are some things your OS should do if it doesn't already. This is a very important step that must be taken before running Lightroom.

Backing Up Your Lightroom Catalog and Images

When you back up your data, it's like safety for your work. Before you update, do these things:

1. Your Lightroom album has all of your changes and settings, so make a copy of it. Open the **Catalog Settings menu** on a PC. To change the catalog settings on a Mac, open **Lightroom Classic.** Click on **Backup Catalog** and pick how often you want to back up.

2. Make a copy of your pictures. To be safe, keep them on a different drive or in the cloud.

The Update Process

Making updates to Adobe Lightroom isn't as hard as it might look. This part will show you a step by step guide so that the update goes quickly and easily.

Navigating the Adobe Creative Cloud for Updates

To begin, to keep Lightroom up to date, you should go to Adobe Creative Cloud. How to get around it:

1. **Open Adobe Creative Cloud:** You can find the Adobe Creative Cloud in the system tray.

2. **Locate Lightroom:** Adobe Lightroom is under Installed Apps in the Apps tab.

3. **Check for Updates:** If there is an update for Lightroom, it will notify you next to it. After that, click **Update**.

   If you can't find the updates, click the **Check for Updates** button. Sometimes it takes a while for things to change.

Troubleshooting Common Update Issues

There may be times when the update process doesn't work right. Why do people often have problems, and how do you fix them?

- **Update not showing:** If the update doesn't show up, make sure the Creative Cloud app is up to date. If not, you should first make changes.

- **Installation errors:** Make sure you can connect to the internet and your device has enough space. It might also help to turn the computer off and on again.

- **Incompatible system:** Remember the check for suitability in the last part? You may need to first make changes to your OS.

Post-Update Steps

There are some important things you should do to make sure everything is working right after you update Adobe Lightroom. You can be sure the update works and quickly get used to the new version if you follow these steps.

Verifying and Testing the Update

After changing, it's important to make sure the new version is in the right place and works as it should. How to do it:

1. **Check the Version:** To see what version you have, open Lightroom and go to **Help > About Lightroom.** This will show you the version number that is being used right now.

2. **Explore New Features:** Read the update notes to learn about any changes or new features. You should give them a try and see how they help you work.

   When you try the software after an update,ensure all the new features work and that your current processes don't change.

Adjusting Settings and Preferences in the New Version

When you get a new update, you may get new choices and some major settings may change. To make them unique:

1. **Review Preferences:** To look over your preferences, go to **Edit > Preferences** on a Windows machine. On a Mac, open **Lightroom** and click on **Preferences**. By clicking on the tabs, you can change settings for speed, layout, and how files are treated.

2. **Update Catalog Settings:** Sometimes updates can change the store settings. When you go to **Edit > Catalog Settings**, you can change how backups, details, and other things are set up.

Lightroom keeps Crashing

Optimize the Catalog

As soon as you choose to improve the catalog, Lightroom will check the data format to make sure it is correct and easy to understand.

Most likely, your store isn't crashing. If it is, though, this should fix it. Also, it will make sure that your catalog works well even after you restart Lightroom.

Click **Optimize Catalog** in the **File** menu after opening the catalog. Give it a moment to work.

After it's done, turn Lightroom back on and see if the problem is still there.

Turn off the GPU

If you've already done steps 1 and 2 and are still having trouble, Lightroom might not be getting along with the driver for your graphics card.

One of the biggest problems for a long time has been graphics card drivers that don't work or are broken with Lightroom. This can lead to slow performance or crashes all the time.

Go to either of these to turn off the **GPU**:

- (Mac) *Lightroom Classic > Preferences > Performance*
- (Windows) *Edit > Preferences > Performance*

Turn off the graphics processor by unchecking the box next to it. The GPU will be turned off. On top of that, this could make Lightroom work faster.

When that doesn't work, you might need to get a GPU that works with Lightroom.

CONCLUSION

To sum up, Adobe Photoshop Lightroom Classic 2025 has a lot of improvements that make it easier and faster to edit and organize pictures. You have more control over your changes with tools like Generative Remove, which is powered by AI, better HDR support, and Denoise for RAW files. It's easier to work with your photos now that tethering works better and the Develop tool runs more smoothly.

No matter how experienced you are as a shooter, these tools will help you get the most out of your photos without making the process too hard. This guide goes over the most important parts of Lightroom Classic that will help you get the most out of it.

INDEX

322

www.ingramcontent.com/pod-product-compliance
Lightning Source LLC
LaVergne TN
LVHW080112070326
832902LV00015B/2551